ti

Dedicated to all who long for a better world.

about
Samuel **Lee**

Samuel Lee is a Pentecostal pastor, evangelist, sociologist, human rights activist, author, and public speaker. He is known for his challenging message on reforming Pentecostalism and for advocating social justice for migrants. He has authored several books such as *Soldier of the Cross, Blessed Migrants, Understanding Japan through the Eyes of Christian Faith* and *Rediscovering Japan, Reintroducing Christendom.*

Dr. Lee founded Foundation University, an online Christian school offering tuition-free education for those who, for economic, political, or religious reasons, are unable to enroll in a course of study elsewhere.

Samuel and his wife, Sarah, live in the Netherlands and serve as pastors among the immigrant and refugee community in Amsterdam.

For more on his life and work visit **samlee**.org.

A **New** Kind of Pentecostalism

A **New** Kind of Pentecostalism

Samuel **Lee**

Foundation University Press
AMSTERDAM

A **New** Kind of Pentecostalism
Promoting Dialogue For Change

second edition

Foundation Press is the non-academic division of Foundation University Press.

Samuel Lee's books may be ordered through booksellers or by contacting:

Foundation Press
Post Office Box 12429
1100 AK Amsterdam, The Netherlands
office@foundationuniversity.com

Unless otherwise noted, all Scripture quotations are from the Holy Bible,

New International Version. ©1973, 1978, 1984, Internationa Bible Society. Used by permission.

Scripture quotations marked AMP are from the Amplified Bible Old Testament. ©1965, 1987 by Zondervan Corporation.

The Amplified New Testament © 1954, 1958, 1987 by the Lockman Foundation. Used by permission.

ISBN: 978-94-90179-19-9

cover photograh | Samuel Lee - *book design* | timmyroland.com

Contents

A **New** Kind of Pentecostalism

Prologue

Current day Christianity is undergoing a serious transition. The global climate is changing quickly, so too with the Christian world. During the course of the last century, the demographic structure of Christianity shifted from its being white dominated to being a colorful mix of races and ethnicities. Now, in the new millennium, Christianity is also changing with respect to its geographic distribution; its epicenter used to be Europe and America, but now it is a "Majority World"[1] religion. These demographic and geographic transitions have also provoked a theological shift. A shift that has been influenced by the new ethnicities in its recipient cultures.

We now portray Jesus not only as a white man with blue eyes, but as a dark skinned African with brown eyes or with any feature of the global family. We speak about African, Asian, and South American Theology, etc. These changes are causing modulations in the culture of Christianity, especially in habits of church going and forms of worship. The white European likes to reason and solemnly worship Jesus on Sundays, the Asian Church, e.g., in Korea, has a Confucian flavor and the African Church prefers to dance and sing in praise. The American Church is a promoter of world evangelization and the expansion of Christianity worldwide but South American Christianity has developed a unique way of combining Catholicism and Pentecostalism.

There are also disadvantages to these powerful demographic and geographic transitions. One of them being that the Church itself is no longer immunized from the risks associated with the

---

1 - The term "Majority World" has here been deliberately chosen as a replacement for "the Third World."

unhealthy elements within every culture.

History proves that, during the period of the early church, the Christian Jews struggled with the Law. Later the Greeks turned Christianity into a Philosophical religion, the Romans institutionalized it, and the Northern and Western Europeans introduced legalism.

Today, whether with conscious intent or not, consumerism has become an influence in the Church in capitalist cultures such as the United States. There everyone seems to strive for everything 'mega': mega church, mega evangelism, mega conversions, etc. People become numbers and 'mega' becomes a sign of success. "Majority World"-Christianity then tries to imitate the American success-oriented Church but often in combination with local magical or shamanistic cultures. The magician is no longer merely a chief, but also a pastor or a prophet—and without the proper training or education. The result is often manipulation, threats and sometimes even very disappointing stories that will be discussed in ensuing chapters. The Pentecostalism in the "Majority World" is producing a novel class of pastors and leaders, nouveau riche, driving limos and flying in helicopters, accompanied by bodyguards, and generally selling success and prosperity, whereas the rest of the population in such countries are struggling with desperate poverty.

If we do not care about this development, if we remain silent in the face of it, then we are allowing Pentecostalism and its institutions to proceed along almost the same lines as Catholicism did in the Middle Ages: selling indulgences, and merchandizing salvation, thus keeping people away from proper Christian education, example, and practice.

The first decade of the new millennium has passed and Pentecostalism is entering into another developmental phase: A New Kind of Pentecostalism. It will be an era of self-evaluation, self-awakening and reform from within. Pentecostalism, with its branches and offshoots, needs reformation and intervention in specific areas where things have gotten out of hand institutionally, and in other areas that have long been neglected.

Before you start reading this book, be aware that I am a Pentecostal, and I have no intention to separate myself from this beautiful and colorful branch of Christianity. On the other hand, I don't believe that Pentecostalism is per se a denomination, but a trans-denominational, trans-geographical, trans-ecclesiastical movement within Christianity in general.

On the other hand, I am a sociologist, so, from the very beginning, I was interested in building a bridge between science and faith. My heart was in social activism and social justice from the early years of my life, even before I met Christ. From a very early age, I was interested in Africa; today I minister predominantly to Africans and Asians.

Despite my enthusiasm, the amazement that miracles provoked in my life and the signs and wonders that I personally experienced, I began to notice that some things are seriously out of balance in our religion. We tend to be overly focused on the miraculous and give less attention to things such as education, character, and personal and institutional integrity. I have experienced people who pray in tongues and fast for days, but often they seemed to care little about personal integrity, moral character, or Christ-like love and compassion. I also noticed how some of us pridefully look down on our brothers and sisters from other denominations.

Over the course of more than two decades of experience in Pentecostalism, I have begun to see that the older this movement is getting, the more it draws on self-imposed laws, self-appointed leaders and self-inspired and self-interest 'revelations.' Many use the Holy Spirit to enrich themselves, become famous, or satisfy their own ego. Think about the exaggerating prosperity preachers, individuals who emotionally manipulate people to give huge amounts of money to their church in order to receive sudden fulfillment of unanswered prayers or achieve miraculous prosperity. All these observations caused me to become ever more committed to scriptural study. There was a passion, a fire burning in me to address certain questions — a kind of response to one hundred years of Pentecostalism. I hope my fellow Pentecostal / Charismatic brothers and sisters will not take the criticisms I articulate here as a personal insult, but rather think about them. They need to give them a hearing so that we can bring this beautiful and colorful Christian movement to fruition.

This book started with an article in my weblog; Post-Pentecostalism. When I wrote it, little did I know that it would produce such a response. I came in contact with people, fellow brothers and sisters within the Pentecostal Movement, who were looking for greater clarity on these questions. It seemed that my article had sparked off something new, something fresh within their souls. Hence the work that you are now holding in your hands.

Eventually I will call this book; "A New Kind of Pentecostalism." I chose "Pentecostalism", because I am referring to the Pentecostal movement as well as many of the organized Pentecostal denominations, which were initiated roughly one hundred years ago. Pentecost on its own is actually the oldest of all Christian movements since it started with Jesus and His disciples, as recorded in the Book of Acts (2); hence it can hardly be new! It is as old as Christianity itself—ancient! Pentecostalism however can persist through every generation; since new generations are always replacing previous ones. However, we as modern day Pentecostals can choose to return to some of the values of Pentecost, as discussed in this work, and thus be renewed by reviving the principles and values found in the book of Acts.

Twenty-first century Pentecostalism needs new ways to approach the intriguing, perplexing, and multidimensional complexity of our world. It has to compete with a multi-faceted world system and offer

Holy Spirit-inspired, practical solutions to the massive stresses our world is subject to. It is time for "A New Kind of Pentecostalism" to develop unique solutions to the crises we face. Everything in our world is now interlinked. Each culture is becoming ever more bound up with the destinies of all of the other world's cultures. Our lifestyle choices on this side of the globe can have a crucial effect on conditions on the other side ecologically, economically, socially or spiritually. Given this fact, we as Pentecostals have to realize that we are a part of a bigger Christian family, a family with two thousand years of history and tradition. This fact alone creates space for dialogue between the people from other denominations or groups who would help us realize that Christianity is more than the interpretation of dogma, or reflection on the Holy Spirit and the scriptures. It is Christ's passion that makes us one, united into a single world community, regardless of denominational background. We are on the verge of something radically new. God is calling His Church to enter into maturity, to demonstrate institutional flexibility, and reveal divine love, to live the credo of tolerance and care for the world. It is my hope that this flame of passion will start burning in you as you read the pages of this book.

This book consists of three parts: part one, The Desire for Balance, deals with some aspects of current day Pentecostalism which need to be addressed; issues such as emotionalism, exaggerations, performance religion, signs and wonders, and idol worshipping in the Church as well as questions of financial ethics and institutional integrity. In part two of this volume, Rethinking our Theology, some themes such as religion, the Holy Spirit, Church, the Kingdom of God, leadership, and the Bible are discussed. The last section, Promoting Change is about the impact Pentecostalism can have on dialogue with other denominations, cultures, and religions. The final chapters of the book describe the crucial role Pentecostalism plays in advocating justice. It stands on the sides of those who are vulnerable and marginalized.

Before undertaking this journey with you, I would like to emphasize that this book has not been written for theologians who study Pentecostalism as a sociological phenomenon in a university setting. It is not a scientific work, but rather written for everyone who has a passion for Pentecostalism. My goal is to be a humble catalyst for change within Pentecostalism. I therefore try to keep my message as simple as possible, to present it in such a way that everyone from every segment of society and every denomination will understand it and be challenged to promote change. So, do not expect to find here an exegesis on Pentecostalism or on the Holy Spirit, or an academic theological work. Rather, this book is written for everyone who is concerned about the current day condition of Pentecostalism.

If we don't attend to the current trends, our mega churches will be leaking people and, within 100 years, these modern institutions will be joining their older 'brothers' in the archives of church history, the records which document the fact that former church buildings have turned into museums and cultural centers. In short, I wrote this book, because I care.

A New Kind of Pentecostalism offers well-intended advice and suggestions for our beautiful Christian movement, hence it is my hope that each chapter of this work will bring about an awakening for those who have lost their way spiritually and provide inspiration to people who have abandoned hope in Pentecostalism.

A **New** Kind of Pentecostalism

A **New** Kind of Pentecostalism

The Desire for **Balance**

part one

A **New** Kind of Pentecostalism

Chapter One

Emotivism

The advantage of the emotions is that they lead us astray.

Oscar Wilde

Our current world is subject to a trend which is actually quite remarkable in human history: the predominance of emotivism— people's feelings, emotions and sensations all seem to be the primary motivating factor in their lives. This is most obvious in public media; music, movies, books, and even news broadcasts. For the past thirty years, our language has been shifting from "I think" to "I believe"— and from "I believe," we are now in the era of "I feel." We usually base our decisions on feelings and say things like; "as long as it feels good and makes you happy, just do it." This is the start of emotivism, and an increasing movement in this direction can only lead to sensationalism and all of the forms of self-indulgence that it implies. Still, this seems to be where our world has now landed in terms of mass psychology. Television reflects this growing trend toward sensationalism in various programs like "Temptation Island" or "Big Brother' and even "Tell-Sell" or "Idols."

Sensationalism has come to dominate not only the media, but other sectors of society as well. In the medical field, for instance, we see increasingly greater variety of drugs available in the free market; the growing demand for plastic surgery is another way to make people feel good about themselves. To make a long story short, it seems that more and more of our daily activities are influenced by human emotions, and the church is no exception to this trend. This is most obvious among Pentecostals, Evangelicals, and the Charismatic churches.

Some Pentecostal gatherings, especially religious conventions, are no longer about preaching a sermon and calling people to God, or edifying the community and praying for the sick, but about show— sound effects, light manipulations, Armani suits, and all forms of glamour. Such displays often are so overwhelming that the attendees can easily be dragged into heightened emotional states. Once I asked a person why he attends a particular church every Sunday and what did he think was so special about it? He answered: "Air conditioning!" At first I did not get it, but then he explained that he visited the church because they have a good air conditioning system. He evidently could not withstand the heat and was bothered by sweating! The church infrastructure made him feel good and comfortable. However, he did not mention anything about the church itself. In that moment I was forced to think about thousands and thousands of fellow Christians in remote areas of Asia or Africa, who don't even have such buildings, and also to think about the persecuted church in the Middle East where people worship God secretly in the deserts, mountains, or caves!

The Pentecostal revival in 1906 was mainly an experience revival rather than a theological one. The outpouring of the Holy Spirit upon the believers in those meetings was rich in love and supernatural manifestations, just as we believe happened on the day of Pentecost in Jerusalem. As the Book of Acts (2) mentions, the apostles and their companions must have looked like drunkards, as they were overwhelmed with the presence of the Spirit. But we forget that right after that powerful experience, after the overwhelming feelings, visceral experience, and the sight of the tongues of fire, the apostle Peter consummated the event with a strong, sound theological sermon. Many times I have attended conferences where the preacher was merely screaming a few words, not delivering a message. No sermon was preached and the little that he did say was driven by mere emotionalism. People got excited and even happy, but they clearly did not hear a divine message from his teaching! This is emotionalism at its worst!

It is certainly true that supernatural experiences get people excited about the gospel, however, over the long term, if these are not combined with education and the cultivation of knowledge, they may cause more damage than blessings. I know many people in my community who have been hurt and confused just because a preacher felt the Holy Spirit telling him something about them. It had huge consequences for their lives. A lady in London, for instance, sold her house and gave it to the preacher; she was clearly being emotionally manipulated. Later she discovered that the preacher divided the money she had donated to him between himself and his two friends for private use.

Such an extremely feeling-oriented Christianity leads us to draw conclusions about people and situations all too easily—and often they are unwarranted. We feel certain things about them. Then we label our feelings as having been sent to us by the Holy Spirit and recount them to the people involved. I once got an email from a Pentecostal brother.

He said that my heart was no longer with the Lord, and that I had forsaken Him—and lots more things. I emailed him back and asked him how he could be so assured that my heart was no more with God. In reply, he said: "I know, because I have the Spirit of God and I feel Him everyday in my heart, so God's Spirit told me that you, Mr. Samuel Lee, are far from living God's will!" Wow! Well, I am strong enough to handle such feeling-based prophecies as they come in through email, but many people are not! They often end up embittered and confused

Experiencing the Holy Spirit and His manifestations can be very beautiful and enriching, but one should not remain on the level of direct experience alone. One needs to move towards deeper understanding of scriptures and their implementation in our daily lives. At times I fear talking to some fellow Pentecostal brothers and sisters about the natural things of life, because almost everything that seems natural may sound to them as if it is from the devil. For example, listening to non-Christian music is a dalliance with evil, as is watching movies.

When we base our lives only on feelings and emotions, we are more prone to be susceptible to fear and manipulation. This may sound familiar to you: sometimes it almost seems like you are sinning because you are not feeling what others feel in a meeting or a conference. "Did you feel the music today?" they ask. Or, they want you to have the same level of enthusiasm as they have about a certain event and when you do not show the emotions they expect to see, they assume that there is something wrong with you. Over the long term, you can even end up as an outcast, literally expelled from the group!

What can we do about the growing emotionalism in the Church? Pentecostalism and all movements committed to biblical Christianity should direct believers to a deeper understanding of the scriptures, but this needs to be combined with the experience of the Holy Spirit. Some of us in the Pentecostal movement lack essential knowledge of what constitutes practice of the faith in a balanced way and we also lack understanding of the scriptures in the context of the global society. Pentecostalism indeed does offer its own theology on the basis of biblical exegesis and guidance in practical matters on the level of the individual, but it gives less attention to essential global and societal matters.

Pentecostal believers seem to know how to pray, attend weekly discipleship meetings, participate in church activities, and attend conferences, and all while their marriages, for example, are falling apart. Perhaps these "spirit-filled" activities are an attempt to escape the stress of real relationships. However, Pentecostalism should approach these issues theologically, systematically, and spiritually—issues such as marriage, family, life, job, city, country, environment, the ecology, etc. It should approach these issues in a balanced and up to date manner! For instance, we have thousands of books written about prosperity and how to be blessed in life, or, how to become rich—to have villas and private jets in the name of the ministry. Yet, far more than half of the Christians in these ministries have large debts and are suffering financially. This is true not only in the developing world, but also in the so-called "First World."

When life is based predominantly on feelings and emotions and people don't make any room for logic or study they often end up making nasty decisions and terrible mistakes. How many times in your life have you given money, donations, or gifts to a ministry because in that moment you felt like giving? That is, without thinking, whether the fundraising is ethical and biblically based or not? Or without asking yourself if you can actually afford to pay that amount of money to the traveling preacher or TV evangelist? Well! I did! I did it in front of the TV! I did it during the conventions! Often, I gave because I was a victim of smooth talk, false hopes, or guilt feelings that were skillfully expressed from the pulpit or in the studio. What happened? I used my credit cards to pay these bills, thereby creating debts for myself at a time when I had no cash or time to do the grocery shopping for my household and kids. The net result was that I ended up almost 10,000 Euros in debt, simply because my giving was based on naiveté and emotional reactions to these pleas.

Consider this example as well: More and more Christians like to experience church in an emotional way. We decorate the podiums with lights and sound systems to give us good and proper feelings. "Goosebumps" are becoming the measure of how good the church service was on Sunday. The pastors begin to compete with each other as to who may be the most Spirit-filled and all of this is judged on the responses of their audiences. Once

I heard several Christians from two different Pentecostal churches disputing—even fighting—about whose church was the best.

Their argument was that the pastor could shout while preaching. They also considered which church service caused more people to fall onto the floor for an "anointing" carpet-time. In other words, what made for an inspiring service was the count of how many people fell down? And these supposedly qualify as arguments? This is what happens, when emotion becomes the value by which all is judged— many, if not most things, including the most important things, will be measured by how they make me feel.

These are only some examples of the unbalanced Christian lifestyle that are causing more troubles in our world day-by-day. Apparently, our so-called super spiritual Pentecostal approach is not working as it should. We need a radical change and more balance in our religious life.

Chapter Two

Exaggerations

An exaggeration is a truth that has lost its temper.

Kahlil Gibran

Exaggeration is another feature of the current Pentecostal movement, one that needs public attention. It is very common among our brothers and sisters. I will never forget the day that a pastor, with whom I was working as a young man, was engaging in such behavior. We were looking for a worship hall for our Sunday services and just about to begin a service ministry which had no more than five to ten members. I accompanied him to visit a hall that could accommodate about five hundred people. The man in charge of the building asked us how large our congregation was. My pastor replied "few thousand." The custodian burst into laughter. Then the pastor told him that he should believe it—we really have thousands of members and on Sundays only a few hundred of them come to this building. I could not believe what I was hearing! When we were in the car, I asked him why he had lied. He told me that I didn't understand the whole thing—he was going on faith, the thousands of members were certain to be there eventually. When I challenged him, he got angry and told me that I had demons inside of me and needed to be exorcised of them. Exaggeration is, in my view, another form of lying. We ought not lie or give false testimony since the Ten Commandments prohibit this.

Exaggeration in numbers

We often exaggerate numbers. I have seen conferences with, let us say, 1500 attendees, and later heard the preacher saying that a few thousand people were present. We also tend to exaggerate the numbers where church membership is concerned. Believe me, I did that too until I was humbled and learned to accept the reality of what I am and what my congregation is. For example, congregations would publicize that they had 500 members attending each Sunday when, in reality, it was only 250 or 300 people. Also previously, when some ministries invited me, they would promise that a couple of thousand people would be attending the conference. But, when I arrived to preach or lecture they had not even mustered a crowd of one hundred.

Exaggeration often happens when we try to impress others. It may also run in parallel with competitiveness. I will never forget a certain moment in my life when I was going through this transformation and humbling process. I was invited to speak at a so-called big conference in a certain Asian country. Upon my arrival, however, I was disappointed to find that there were only eight people there on the first night. It was next to impossible to conduct the service because of my disappointment. When I went to my room to pray, God spoke to my heart through His scriptures and reminded me not to despise such small numbers. He also reminded me that regardless of how many people were in attendance, those who were present were human beings and God cared for each of them individually. That night I cried and wept before God on account of my wicked ego and my performance-oriented ministry. I repented and asked His Spirit to create in me a clean, humble heart. Next day there was again a group of only ten to fifteen people attending. I began to preach. While I was doing so, a woman began to weep deeply. I did not know that she had also been there the day before. She came and testified that she had been about to commit suicide yesterday, and someone had brought her to the conference. God saved her from doing this. In my room I prayed again and this came to my mind: "you see I just came here for that one soul." We often like exaggeration and big crowds, but God looks at the hearts of individuals.

We exaggerate our reports of miracles and healing

I do believe in signs and wonders, and so agree that they are still a reality in our modern world. In my view, the traditional church and other established denominations should take more seriously the practice of healing and praying for the sick. In my ministry I have often experienced miracles and still witness them today. In 1999 I was in Conakry, the capital city of Guinea, West Africa, a predominantly Muslim nation. They had leased an empty field in which I was to conduct a conference. One day, a Christian police officer came to my hotel secretly. He begged me not to conduct the conference that night because some people had threatened that they would kill many participants, including the speaker. I did not know what to do. I prayed and then went to the conference nevertheless and began to preach. It was dark. A small generator provided electricity and it clearly did not suffice for such a big place. The lights went out, and my microphone was not working properly. While I was preaching, I saw at the far back of the field a group of people running towards the podium. I was terrified and so were my two interpreters.

It seemed like the moment of my death was impending. As the crowd was approaching, I saw an old man running out ahead of them. At that moment, someone came and whispered in my ears: "the guy who is running was a paralyzed man and while he was listening to your message a miracle took place. He jumped out of his wheelchair and started to run. When people saw him, those who knew who he was began to run after him in joy and excitement." So, yes, I do still believe in miracles and am sure that God uses me to aid many. But, I have to admit that I have also prayed for people who were not healed, in fact some of them even died. Nevertheless, some were indeed made whole again. Some European countries plan to forbid pastors and clergy to pray for the sick due to unreality about healing.

Some pastors who pray for the sick tell the patients that they either have been or will be healed. So, people come to believe that they don't need doctors or medical help anymore. They profess that their faith has healed them. Unfortunately some have died and so the authorities are now investigating the possibilities of forbidding such practices. I know for instance in some African countries, where Pentecostalism is strong, that the preachers pray for HIV infected people and assure them that they will be healed by "faith." The results are deeply problematic: these men or women continue to infect others, while under the illusion that God has already healed them.

We are out of balance with respect to spirituality and religiosity

Have you met people who try to impress you with their spirituality and spooky stories? Well, I have! Lots of Christians don't seem to be able to live without such excesses. Some of them come to my office to connect with me, or they need me for one reason or another. As soon as they enter the office, they attempt to impress me with their stories of "being in the Spirit." One lady mentioned the names of all the demons in her town and explained how she chased them away by means of fasting and prayer. She told me how she was called up into third heaven like the apostle Paul—and many other similar stories. All of this was said just to impress me, to show me how spiritual she was. Unfortunately, this "spiritual" woman—herself a pastor—had such serious problems in her marriage and with her sons that her husband left her and took his sons with him.

Another excess we often get involved in concerns religiosity. I will never forget a time that I had to give counsel to a married couple where the wife remembered her pastor's birthday but forgot her own husband's! Often, we can be so busy in the ministry, praying, fasting, serving in the church, and being involved with all forms of excessive religious activity that we neglect the very essential matters of life, such as family.

I often travel to the beautiful country of Korea. There I have asked many believers to tell me what is important in their Christian life. Almost 80 percent reply: God, Church, and family—and most of them are women, who serve in the church, cooking and doing administration. They often neglect their husbands, coming home late from work or prayer meetings. Tomorrow a conference is scheduled and the next day, a bible study session. No wonder the husband ends up either meeting other women, or addicted to pornography, alcohol, or drugs. I met one such individual whose son tried to commit suicide because mom and dad were so often at church rather than at home.

If we want this Pentecostal movement to succeed, we have to do something about our tendency to excess. It is my hope that, as New Pentecostals, we can address these issues and teach our congregations to avoid excess in pseudo-spiritual, religious activity.

A **New** Kind of Pentecostalism

Chapter Three

Performance

*Bullfighting is the only art in which the artist is in danger
of death and in which he degree of brilliance in the performance
is left to the fighter's honor.*

Ernest Hemingway

The current world crisis which humanity has created for itself demands maximum performance from all of us. The capitalist societies and open-market economies have led us to create a world that is extremely competitive. While competition can certainly lead to improved performance, the desire for success can also become an obsession. People are forced to be fake, and out of touch with their own reality.

The Pentecostalism of the twenty-first century, especially in the West, is infected with this "performance-virus." Suddenly, our success is being measured in terms of the church membership counts, or the size of church buildings, or the preacher's 'performance' and tithing. It all seems to be no longer about souls, but about numbers: How many people attended the conference? Or the church service? In the late '80s, we were satisfied with ten thousand attendees at a conference, but, by the end of the '90s, prominent Pentecostal leaders spoke about crusades with two to three hundred thousand participants. Now at the beginning of the new millennium, even these numbers no longer satisfy us! We have begun to whisper that the attendees number in the millions! However, despite all these attendees, Africa is still battling AIDS, poverty, and ethnic cleansing!

The New Pentecostalism should not focus on numbers alone, but on fellowship of the human spirit with God, on the breaking of bread with our fellow human beings.

We seem to have forgotten that we are human!

As a pastor, I have to confess that there is an increasing demand for me to perform! People expect me to work miracles, or to reveal a prophetic message. They forget though that man cannot do these things—only God can. There was a time in which I was very tired of having this demand placed on me. Believers and conference attendees expect me to be a super, ultra, mega powerful "man of God." Fewer people seem to be interested in my life as a father, brother, husband, friend or neighbor, much less as a follower of the Way!

On the other hand, the post-modern, non-religious society is not interested in our evangelistic flyers, tracks, and church bulletins. They need to see us Christians as human beings, as ordinary people who may possess extraordinary spiritual energy. Once I asked a group of believers, "Who are you?" and the majority replied, "We are Christians." Some responded that they were "children of God," and others mentioned "Pentecostals." Their replies made me think how far removed we are from our basic humanity! No one thought to reply that he/she was first a human being. Maybe it seems to readers that it is quite odd for someone to remark on this, but, really, it is natural that we first acknowledge our humanity.

In the Hebrew language, the word "Adam" means man or human. In the Middle East, we refer to all human beings as Adam. These days I am beginning to grasp a very important fact, namely, that I am a human being before I am a Christian. A human being! Only now, am I starting to realize this simple, yet powerful truth.

Reading the first chapters of Genesis reminds us that God created Adam and Eve, and that He made man in His own image. We are beings that He loves and He cares for. He did not create Christians in the beginning, but Adams—human beings. And, God created mankind for this purpose—to be human. Alas, we are not angels, nor are we spirits! After the fall of man in Genesis, humanity became fragile, weak, corrupt, and sinful. At the same time, however, we possessed goodness, kindness, righteousness, and love—but not a complete love. Jesus Christ came into this world to reconcile us to the Father and help us to restore the humanity within us; to restore to us the humanity that was supposed to be ours, but was lost in the Garden of Eden. Still, we are all on the way, all moving toward that day when we will be fully restored to that level of humanity. As long as we are here on earth, though, sharing the planet with almost 8 billion neighbors, we must remain cognizant of the human aspects of our being.

At this historical moment, unfortunately, some of us have created an elite group called super Christians. This group assumes that God only cares for them and no one else—they are Daddy's special kids. What are the consequences of such thinking? We become arrogant and consider others as nobodies, treat them as gentiles or pagans. We act as if we are the only ones on the planet earth for whom God cares. This is nothing short of Pharisee-ism! Do you recall the story of Nicodemus, who went to Jesus at night so as to become part of God's kingdom? Jesus challenged this Pharisee to become born again through the spirit of God; then, in John 3:16, Jesus immediately proclaimed, "For God so loved the world that He gave His Son." In other words, He urged Nicodemus to stop treating people as dogs, and to treat them as human beings in so far as He reminded him that God loves the entire world and not just a particular group of religious people. If we realize that we are human beings who have been given a divine revelation in the form of Christ, then we are able to manifest the love of God to others in a genuine and caring way.

Focusing on how to perform Christianity, rather than on being a follower of Christ—being simply a human being—turns us into a ministry-driven people. We become performers of Christianity rather than followers of Christ. I now understand that before being a pastor I am a father and a husband. My wife doesn't need a pastor; she needs a husband. My children do not need a preacher in the house; they need a father. We have to realize that before being a participant at a Sunday morning fellowship, we are someone's neighbors. Before we possess right religiosity and sound dogma, we ought to have a human heart. We do have to live life and enjoy it—celebrate it as human beings who exist in the fullness of Christ Jesus.

In Ephesians the Apostle Paul writes about five-fold ministry:

It was he (Christ) who gave some to be apostles, some to be prophets, some to be pastors and teachers, to prepare God's people for works of service, so that the body of Christ may be built up until we all reach unity in the faith and in the knowledge of the Son of God and become mature, attaining to the whole measure of the fullness of Christ.

Ephesians 4:11-13

Inspired by Paul, I believe in the five-fold ministry of life: "And some God made them parents (fathers & mothers), children (sons & daughters), some siblings (brothers/sisters), some spouses (husbands & wives) & some He made to be friends (neighbors) in order for us to make a better world, to build each other up and help each other to make God's dream become reality." Unless we take as our starting point such genuine ministries of life any other systematic theology or doctrinal study matters less—or perhaps not at all!

Our overemphasis on performance causes us to wear masks and these portray us as "supermen"—individuals without any weaknesses and frailties. We do this because many of us are actually suffering inside. We have lots of questions and are subject to many temptations. We cannot talk to our fellow Christians, because of the severity of the potential social consequences: isolation, judgment, and gossip. Why do some of us leaders and clergy fall into the sin of adultery? Because we are lonely! Because we pretend, we act as if we are the strong men of God and ideal Christians, and no one expects us to be weak. But we have issues in the area of personal finance, sexuality, and leadership, and we may not be able to speak out about them. We are beset with many serious struggles and questions.

God chose to become human. How much more should we be human! A good friend of mine once said: "Jesus did not come as a Christian; He came as a human." The Word became flesh! (John 1). Jesus came to restore us to Adamhood! To be a human being helps us to express the love of God and the good news of Jesus Christ much more effectively than does possession of any doctrinal formula or any professional ministry personae.

I have also begun to realize that the people of the world do not always reject the gospel of Jesus Christ, but often they simply do not understand it! Why? Simply because they are human beings. It is not easy to understand it if one lacks personal conviction. What if your wife were to come to you one day and say, "Honey, I am pregnant, but not by you. The Spirit of God created a child in me." What would you think? The first thing that comes to my mind would be the need for a DNA test! So, how in the world can we expect people to believe the story of the annunciation and the virgin birth? This is a feat that is entirely beyond human powers. Moreover, how can people believe in the resurrection? It is beyond the scope of human reason. Still, if we do not understand something, that does not mean we ought to reject it. As noted, the majority of the world population has probably not rejected the gospel; they simply have not understood it. Why? There are many possible reasons. First, understanding it requires that we get beyond the powers of human reason, beyond all of the restrictions that our very nature places upon us. But, also, some claim not to be able to understand the gospel because of the corruption they have seen in Christians. How in the world do we expect people to convert to Christianity when the news broadcasts detail the cynical and sometimes criminal ways that religious leaders behave? When church buildings are replete with gold and silver, while elsewhere masses of people are suffering from hunger? When Christians justified slavery until almost two hundred years ago? Or when superstar TV preachers enrich themselves at the cost of crisis-stricken people, ruthlessly relieving them of their last penny? Or, when something so heinous as child molestation occurs in God's sanctuaries? All of these failings reveal only that we are human beings, no better than people of any other religious group! I really believe that there are people in the world who are in love with Jesus and His teachings, but actually they do not understand Christians and Christianity. One day a close family member said to me while watching a screaming TV preacher in an Armani suit demand money from his listeners, "Sam, I love Jesus, but please don't turn me into someone like that," pointing her finger at the evangelist.

When we show the world that we as Christians are human beings, that we, too, have emotions, feelings, make mistakes, and experience joy, happiness, sorrow, etc.; when the people of the world notice our humanity and humility, then the Holy Spirit will convince them of the importance of the message of Jesus Christ! Let us be first friends, neighbors, brothers, sisters, sons or daughters. Let us not be mere actors lost in lies and duplicity.

The people of the world are not naïve and godless even though we often portray them that way. They know what is genuine and what is not! If we, as Pentecostal believers, ever want to reach the internet-generation, the Green Peace generation, MTV/TMF men and women, and, if ever we want be members of the highly informed and rapidly changing global village, then we have to be real, consistent and honest! Let us be human first and foremost, and manifest Jesus' love through our humanity as the Holy Spirit inspires us to do! I know many are offended by my words, but it is my hope that many

Chapter Four

Miracles, Signs & Wonders

*The miracle is not to fly in the air, or to walk
on the water; but to walk on the earth.*

A Chinese Proverb

The verse "Jesus Christ is the same yesterday, today & forever" (Hebrews 13:8) is one of the most quoted biblical texts among Pentecostal believers. One of the core principles of our Pentecostal religion is a belief in the miraculous; the faith in Jesus Christ's ongoing ability to perform miracles through the faithful. There is absolutely no doubt about the miracles performed today. But, my concern in this work centers more on commercialization of the miraculous and overemphasis on signs and wonders. It is as if signs and wonders are the only concerns people have about Jesus Christ. There are some angles we have to consider when it comes to such things.

The Individualistic Angle

Individualism is a rapidly growing social phenomenon that seems to become more problematic with the economic growth and the increasing greed that accompanies it. Within the Pentecostal movements, there is a seeming tendency for God to continually bless the individual, even if it is to the disadvantage of others. Once I was chatting with a fellow Pentecostal, who was telling me how exited he was about a miracle he experienced. They had a barbeque party and invited others to join for prayer and fellowship. However, it started to rain. He explained excitedly: "And we prayed to God to stop the rain in Jesus name. Guess what? The rain stopped." Whether God listened to their prayers or not, one thing is sure the rain stopped! However, my friend's prayer shows a certain degree of individualistic longing for miracles that serve only him and his guests. How about others who are in need of rain? How about the nature? How about the farmers who needed rain?

Consider this: Most of the wishes we express for miracles on Christian TV are about how to get rich, be blessed, own a bigger house, etc. It's all about ME! These are purely selfish desires! I am not against such prayers at all. Indeed, I am sure those who need these things may have their own legitimate reasons as to why they pray for them. However, we have to place miracles in the right perspective. They express God's glory, love, and care for mankind and creation. They help us to manifest His love and bring others closer to His heart. Whether a crippled child is healed instantly through prayer or gradually through the work of a doctor, a miracle has occurred.

Some Pentecostals seem to get chills from watching exciting miracle shows on Christian media. It may be great to see, but I would argue that the New Kind of Pentecostalism needs to move beyond this and enter into the sign and wonder of love, per se: the miracle of caring for one another in the Spirit of Christ.

Further, I am concerned that we are so preoccupied with looking for miracles or chasing after signs and wonders that we forget to look at the daily miracles of life all around us. Miracles are relative to time and space. Something that we called a miracle two hundred years ago is already a normal happening today. Air travel is a case in point. A few hundred years ago, no one could believe this was possible. It was regarded as a potential miracle. Today, thousands and thousands of flights are flown everyday all around the globe. God gave man the ability to explore, to discover, to invent. This is not a miracle, strictly speaking. Yet, all of what man has is from God.

Being alive, existing, breathing, loving and being loved—these are all miracles and the type we tend to overlook. We seem to be in search of gold dust on our bodies during a Pentecostal conference,[1] precious stones that appear in the sanctuary, or diamonds in the churchyard. These are all nice to hear about and may be even to experience, but, as noted, I believe, as a Pentecostal, that we have to go back to our roots and pray for the sick and aid the needy. This is what Jesus demanded from His disciples; to pray for the sick, heal and care for people, and to expel evil. He asked that we do all these things in His name and in a way that reflects His character.

The Commercial Angle

During past decades, the work of performing miracles has been turned in to a business involving billions of dollars. I call it, for lack of a better name, the Miracle Industry. The commerce in Pentecostal / Charismatic books on how to receive miracles, and how to get rich through them constitute a billion dollar industry. At times Christian television is one of its most avid promoters: make a donation to such and such a ministry and within a certain time frame you can expect to experience your miracle. "Act now" they advertise "and you will see your miracle." I even heard a preacher saying, "God can even stop the earth from turning for your sake alone!" But, really, we cannot—and may not—commercialize the miracles of the Holy Spirit. As a new kind of Pentecostal, I am seeking justice. We must speak out against this abuse but do so in the spirit of Christian love. We must express our concern about this 'Industry' particularly, given that it has so strongly linked prosperity to the gospel message. I address this problem in the next chapter.

Unfortunately, commercialization of miracles has also created a group of Christians who are willing to buy theirs, i.e., to pay a certain

---

1 - In some Pentecostal gatherings, some people claim that God has given certain individuals gold teeth and/or that He exchanges their regular, amalgam fillings for gold fillings. Some experience the appearance of gold dust on their clothing and some find precious stones in the conference halls or church sanctuary. I absolutely am not speaking against such manifestations and I cannot judge such events. However, I do not consider them as the most important thing in the Pentecostal movement.

ministry in order to get some miraculous benefit—and this without making any effort themselves. They merely wait for God to intervene in their lives. They sit at home and have no motivations to help themselves. They build up more debt and simply hope that one day a miracle will occur and release them from all of it!

The Witchcraft Angle

Exaggerated and excessive claims about miracles are leading some Pentecostals into what I call "witchcraft"—and this in the name of Jesus. This is a new phenomenon among the Western churches, but quite an old one among the non-Western Pentecostals. Lack of spiritual education motivates some groups of Pentecostals to pray for the death of their enemies. In some churches, they call this "shooting time:" praying, in Jesus' name, for the demise of someone whom they do not like! The way they perform such a spiritual shooting event is absolutely silly: they take their Bibles in hand as if they are holding a shotgun, then, when the preachers tell them to imagine their enemy, they mention the name. When the preacher gives the go ahead, they all shout and aim their Bibles at their enemies in the "Spirit." A sad story indeed.

Others pray for marriages, or for the breakup of relationships in order that someone else may get involved. Pathetic, really, but such things are happening in some of our Pentecostal churches. Once I heard a certain pastor proclaiming that if we do not pray for the death of our enemies, they will kill us, instead. I thought he meant "devils" or "evil spirits," but later I understood that by 'enemy' he literally meant other human beings.

No doubt, many Pentecostals would never do such things; however, it is important to be aware of the existence of such practices. Pentecostalism is about saving, not killing! About forgiving, not hating; preserving, not destroying.

Chapter Five

Financial Ethics

"Dear Prosperity Preachers and all those who preach about how God wants you to be rich: Since you already have millions of dollars it seems that you are always short on money. You keep asking for people to send 'faith seeds' so you can send them "real anointing oil" from the holy land in a little vile for $5 when you can buy a whole bottle of extra-virgin for $10 from Coles. It's time for you all to put your money where your mouth is. I have an answer to your financial need so you can make another $100 million dollars in this financial year. You seem to talk a lot about the parable of the sower, where you sow something and you'll get 10 or 100 fold back. So, here's what I want you to do . . . Please send me $1000 and you can have the $100,000 God will send you in return." [1]

Michael Elliot, blogger

Michael is only one example of thousands of people who have questions about the way Pentecostals preach about finances. Internet is full of comments and blogs about this type of things. I personally believe that we have to reform the way we deal with finances, particularly where fundraising and the accumulation of tithes and offerings are concerned! Most Pentecostal ministries fail miserably in this area! There are lots of generous donors among Pentecostals but sadly, they themselves often end up suffering financially. We live in an age of easy access to credit, high technology and the speedy flow

1 - Taken from Michael Elliott's Blog: "The Mick's Grill: Tasty Servings of Pop Cultures & Nonsense" August 9, 2010. http://micksgrill.wordpress.com/2010/08/09/dear-prosperity-gospel-preachers/

of information through various means. Often times, TV evangelists' gospel programs cause confusion among their listeners as to where to send their gifts and offerings. Easy credit card use causes people to become lightheaded and negligent, and to end up in serious debt. Emotional manipulation leads to a 'merchandizing' of the Holy Spirit. Worldly, and highly questionable, techniques are applied to accumulate money for the "ministry."

I myself have attended conferences and meetings at which the preacher urged the people that if they wanted to be debt-free within a certain amount of time, they should invest a certain amount of money, often large, into his ministry. This is hardly appropriate for a man of God! At the same time these individuals talk publicly about their villas and Rolex watches while they continue to say that they need money for the 'ministry.' It mystifies me why some religious leaders need to stay in hotels that cost 10,000 Euros per night – and then ask for still more money for their ministry. Something is terribly wrong here!

During the past twenty years, and especially the last decade, the "Prosperity Gospel" is becoming more and more popular in Charismatic / Pentecostal circles. In this chapter, I am therefore sharing some of my concerns about this false gospel and its methods of fundraising. I will also be recounting some of my own experiences, and suggesting how we, as Christians, can bring back balance to our religious lives. I will also be addressing what I take to be some of the root causes of this phenomenon. Lastly, let me make it clear to all concerned that it is absolutely not my intention to attack or in any way harm the Pentecostal / Charismatic movement. As noted, I myself am a member of it. Rather, my purpose is to raise some serious questions regarding what I take to be some of the problematic practices in today's Church. Solutions must be forthcoming. It is my hope that this work will contribute to them.

Blessings Theology - Prosperity Gospel

There is a very crucial distinction to be made here between Blessing Theology and the Prosperity Gospel. Blessing Theology is about messages, teachings and ministry as it focuses on the blessed aspects of life: it holds that it is everyone's right to live a blessed life, as given by God, including enjoying blessings in the areas of family, career, marriage and finances. This can be achieved by obeying God's commands, following the scriptures and committing to hard work. This may seem to be a kind of Calvinistic view, but Blessing Theology is very successful in the Majority World where people are looking for hope and improvement in their life circumstances. A great example of such Blessing Theology is to be found in Dr. David Y. Cho's approach in South Korea. Dr. Cho started his ministry in the 1950s in the slum areas of Seoul. During those days Korea was a very poor nation. His theology was based on "Blessings." His sermons promoted a blessed lifestyle. Today, Dr. Cho has one of the largest churches in the world, the Yoiddo Full Gospel Church, with 750 thousand members. His theology has inspired and greatly affected the members of this church. Many of them were initially poverty-stricken, but today they are very successful businessmen.

The Prosperity Gospel stands in sharp contrast to this. It is very materialistically motivated. The core of its message is devotion to Mammon. It focuses on obtaining money, wealth and power over the short term with the help of the Holy Spirit's intervention. How did this troublesome trend start?

During the '90s, and especially the first decade of the new millennium, mega-churches, mega-preachers and TV evangelists became more popular day by day. Those who had money got on TV and in the print media, no matter what they were preaching. This created a new elite within the Christian world: superstar pastors and leaders who displayed their glamour and mystical charisma on TV. These electronic evangelists then became the heroes of the Christian masses.

In order to stay in the spotlight, many of these superstar preachers needed money. Gradually, a whole marketing industry was created, one that specialized in developing mass communication strategies. Also, a new type of theology was formed: the Prosperity Gospel. It preaches that God wants you to be rich, to have lots of goods and things. God wants you to dress in the most expensive brands and drive the most exclusive cars. But there is a catch: In order to achieve this, one must "invest" in "God's Kingdom;" and most of the time "God's Kingdom" was equivalent to the Superstar's own ministry. Only then can the "wealth anointing" power of the evangelist—the supposed man/woman of God—also flow to the giver. Such a theology of prosperity is nothing but a form of theologized gambling! One risks one's money with the hope of gaining over the short term what was invested over the long term. The Prosperity Gospel's deepest roots reach down into our materialistic worldview. Unlike the Blessing Theology, which only focuses on paying tithes and offerings and living a holy life, the Prosperity Gospel involves manipulation. Such pastors not only demand tithes and offerings, but also gifts and 'seeds.' Most of these Prosperity preachers have serious moral and ethical problems.

I invite you to participate in an exciting experiment. If you have access to satellite TV or the Internet, please watch the Christian TV channels over the course of a day. You will be shocked and perplexed to see how fundraising is conducted by some of these individuals. Lots of noise, lots of big promises, and then the preacher demands that the viewer run and pick up the phone within 5 to 10 minutes, and only during this 5 to 10 minute time period. If the viewer calls and donates a certain amount of money, then, miraculously, a blessing or a miracle will be released to them within a designated time period. This is nothing short of fraud. This is internet gambling in the name of religion!

During the '90s, these superstar pastors used satellite TV to display their glamour to the Majority World. They became a source of inspiration and an ultimate model for many ministers in the Majority World, e.g., Africa, Asia, South America. Lots of ministers started imitating Hollywood Christianity and they dreamed of developing similar ministries. The problem here was that they did not live in the USA, but in poverty-stricken parts of the world. How could they become successful if their people were living in poverty? But, even more important to note is the fact that the Prosperity Gospel is not bound to a specific country or region of the world. It is everywhere, and, during times of economic malaise, it seems still more appealing.

In the following case studies, I deliberately do not mention names or specific locations. I have nothing against the people involved, but I do strongly disapprove of the way they conduct their ministries. Also, this discussion need not degenerate into a bout of name calling or personality conflicts. Nevertheless, what you will read below will rend your heart!

I know of one well-known Christian leader, who owns private jets, a couple of villas, hundreds of hand-made suits and 12 Rolex watches. He also publicly discusses his wealth—in detail. He claims that others, too, can become like him—they only need supernatural wisdom. Then he asks who wants his wealth anointing to transfer to them. Of course, people get very excited. They all want such opulence. He then asks them to come forward and requests 100 US$ for each member of a family. In other words, if you are a family of four, you then had to pay $400. In a conference with 2000 people, how much money would this bring in? Subsequent to this, he claims that those who invest this money will be rich within one hundred days. Many people do make such payments, and after one hundred days nothing happens.

I will never forget a Pentecostal preacher who conducted a three-night conference. I was in attendance. He started preaching about how God has blessed him in Africa, how rich he is and how God has anointed him. As he continued his message, the focus of the sermon gradually shifted towards money. At the end he said: "This morning I was praying and the Holy Spirit was very strong in my hotel room." He then explained, "The Holy Spirit urged me to ask you tonight, if there are 100 people in this room who need a financial miracle." He continued: "If each one of you plant a seed of 2000 Euros in my ministry, this breakthrough will come to you before the end of the year." He even urged people to borrow from others in order to be able to donate such an amount. What truly saddened me is that his audience was composed of suffering migrants, people from the most vulnerable segments of society. He was bilking them of their resources, just like the Pharisees who deceived the poor widow in the temple into giving them her last coin.

"As he taught, Jesus said, "Watch out for the teachers of the law. They like to walk around in flowing robes and be greeted with respect in the marketplaces, 39 and have the most important seats in the synagogues and the places of honor at banquets. 40 They devour widows' houses and for a show make lengthy prayers. These men will be punished most severely."

Mark 12:30-40

There are far too many examples to share here. A traveling prophet asked those who wanted to dine with him and receive a personal prophesy to pay $1500 US (per person) in order to be allowed to sit at his left or right hand.

Another traveling prophet conducted a conference, during which he explained that the Holy Spirit had anointed him and had asked him to distribute salt to the people. Anyone who bathed in it would receive a miracle and could even become a millionaire. The only thing the attendants had to do was buy a glass full of salt for 1000 Euros. If people did not have that much cash on hand he was "gracious enough" to give a discount of 100 Euros per spoonful. There are still many more examples I can cite to unmask the bald-faced injustice and manipulation that has become a hallmark of our Church's financial system: Robbing widows of their homes and plundering the resources of the suffering in the name of God and prosperity.

Pentecostal churches that are involved in such practices should cease and desist from them! All forms of ungodly and inappropriate fundraising, particularly where emotional manipulation is involved, are fundamentally wrong. It was certainly never Christ's intention to manipulate people in order to collect donations, offerings, or tithes. But, today, a vital economy has grown up around these unsavory practices. Ministers and ministries who engage in such types of fundraising should commit to a lifestyle that conforms to ministerial ethics. In other words, one cannot demand sums of money from people and at the same time live a life of luxury. Such people are hardly men or women of God. Christian leaders should stop focusing on wealth and enriching themselves at the expense of the church and the ministry. Instead, they should publicly confess their sins and return to an authentic and humble Christian lifestyle. Does this mean that I am against wealth? No, not at all. I am opposed to wrongheaded methods of acquiring it, in particular, the use of the ministry for this purpose. And even if funds are legitimately raised for the ministry, men of God should use them not to enrich themselves, but for the purposes for which they were intended, namely for the salvation of souls and the betterment of the community.

Tithes & Offering

In Pentecostal churches, the following Old Testament text is often cited to indicate that those who do not pay their tithes are robbing God:

"I the LORD do not change. So you, the descendants of Jacob, are not destroyed. Ever since the time of your ancestors you have turned away from my decrees and have not kept them. Return to me, and I will return to you," says the LORD Almighty. "But you ask, 'How are we to return?' "Will a mere mortal

rob God?" Yet you rob me. "But you ask, 'How are we robbing you?'"In tithes and offerings. You are under a curse—your whole nation—because you are robbing me. Bring the whole tithe into the storehouse, that there may be food in my house. Test me in this," says the LORD Almighty, "and see if I will not throw open the floodgates of heaven and pour out so much blessing that there will not be room enough to store it. I will prevent pests from devouring your crops, and the vines in your fields will not drop their fruit before it is ripe," says the LORD Almighty."Then all the nations will call you blessed, for yours will be a delightful land," says the LORD Almighty."

Malachi 3:6-12

We often place a burden of guilt and fear upon people when they do not pay their tithes and make their offerings. Have you yourself ever experienced, for example, when your car is damaged or your glasses are suddenly broken, that some religious people directly connect that with your not having paid your tithes? And, "You may not have, but I have!" Even I have preached such stuff before! However, this kind of message does not fit with the New Testament image of God. When we compare God the Father to a loving human father how can an earthly father ask his children to pay him a tenth of their pocket money, then claim that he will give them more? And, this on the basis that he will punish and curse them if they do otherwise? If I as a father perform such an act, and my children report it to the police with evidence, I would surely be arrested and accused of extortion. No doubt, the words I am writing here will not be welcomed in many churches. Some readers may even close this book at this point and stop reading it altogether. But, I am convinced that tithes and offering should not be requested using coercive methods.

Giving should be done on the basis of grace, out of a sense of true generosity, not fear. Unfortunately, some of our colleagues and brethren have created a theology of fear when it comes to these matters. Still, God's message is not about a curse, but about a blessing. There is no condemnation for those who believe: He has paid our debts with His life, death and resurrection. An individual who tithes with genuinely good intentions and a good heart will surely be blessed, but someone who does not tithe will surely not be cursed!

The word 'tithing' is not even mentioned once in the New Testament. However, I do understand that organized churches ask for tithes and offerings for practical reasons. They have many bills to cover, e.g., building construction and maintenance, electricity, costs associated with mission work, salaries of those who serve the church full time, etc. This is all understandable. As long as one is a member of such a church, then one has to share in its burdens. As a general rule, we cannot benefit from membership in a community unless we contribute to it. But this does not mean that the pastor or the elders have to preach fear and guilt in order to cover the costs of their ministries. All they need to do is ask people for assistance, honestly outline the needs of the church.

We cannot arbitrarily accept some truths of the Old Testament and reject others. Either we have to believe all of what it says, or we have to concede that no one can follow the law in its fullness and we are therefore in need of God's grace. The Apostle Paul mentions that the law will judge those who follow it. If we, in this Era of Grace, choose to follow it, we will be judged by it. Therefore, if we preachers instill fear in our congregations when it comes to tithing, we then subject our selves and our listeners to the curse of the law.

A **New** Kind of Pentecostalism

Chapter Six

Idol Worship of the Church

Americans are good at democracy, and their ideal government
is a government without a king. But although they dislike kings
and emperors, they live like kings and emperors.

Uchimura Kanzo[1] (1861-1930)

I used to ridicule my Catholic brothers and sisters and accuse them of idol worship. "They have lots of idols in their sanctuaries" I said. I also used to make fun of my Greek Orthodox friends, because I thought they were worshiping the icons in their churches. How foolish and how shortsighted of me! One day, when I was praying and meditating, a little voice inside me showed me my hypocrisy. It whispered, "You too are an idol worshipper!" then continued, "You are an idol worshipper. You don't worship idols of stone but you worship living idols, idols with flesh and blood." "Who then?" I asked myself. The voice in my mind said: "you worship famous men and women in ministry. At times you even esteem them higher than Jesus. You do all you can to see them, meet them. You get excited when you attend their conferences and have contact with them." The voice was right. In the Catholic Church, they may have statues that represent the saints of the old and the apostles, but the idols I was admiring and worshipping were the living kings of the church.

The success stories of ministries in combination with Christian media have created an elite group of Christian leaders, a sort of nouveau riche leadership and we have crowned them as our kings.

---

1 - Kanzo, Uchimura. "Can Americans Teach Japanese in Religion?" Japan Christian Intelligencer 1, no. 9
(5 November 1926), in Works, 30:98-105.

Who do we really follow as a Church or a ministry? Do we follow the example of these so-called successful tele-evangelists, or that of Jesus, our Lord? What is the standard by which we measure our success? What exactly are we achieving? Is it true success? Jesus was a different kind of a leader, a different kind of a King!

Today, we tend to place our leaders on the thrones. Jesus, however, did not have a throne when He was on earth. His only possession was the Cross-and His only crown was one made of thorns. What a King we have! Many of us who are religious leaders are far, far from accepting the cross as our throne. Instead, we have chairs painted gold, and place them on a podium for when the 'king' appears! The pastor sits there as if he were a king, far from his people isolated in the pride which "goes before the fall."

Disobeying religious authority has now become directly related to sinning against God. Often in churches it is quoted "Do not touch my anointed ones."(Psalm 105:15). Any criticism one receives tends to derive from this and it is thought that it can have fatal spiritual consequences. But, Jesus Christ, King of Kings, chose to be punished in our place. He chose to die for all of mankind. He chose death that we may live.

The idols that we worship today are so detached from people that even to succeed in physically touching them would be an achievement. Some of them even walk around with bodyguards. However, for me, they are no longer models of spirituality. They have become models of monstrous religiosity. I prefer instead to go directly to Christ, to follow His example. Jesus chose to associate with all men, rich or poor. One day, He ate at the home of some prominent men in Jerusalem and the other day He was walking with 5000 poor people, feeding them. He was not ashamed to talk to a prostitute and call her His sister, or to walk with a traitor like Zaccheus, or to eat a meal as a homeless person.

Jesus the King is the lover of all people. The golden crowns, rings, luxury 'watches' and the wealth of the world, did not impress Him. He could see right through all of these expensive attempts to cover mortal flesh, and see into the heart of man, where everyone is naked, fragile and hiding from something. Whether people were rich or poor, Jesus was able to reach them all during His time here on earth. The royalty of this world prefer to associate with their own groups of people, based on race, economic status and cultural background. Jesus, however, did not look at a person's denominational affiliation or cultural background. Instead, He reached them all with His kind words and love. I am sure if He were on earth today, He would maintain fellowship with a Muslim, love a Buddhist and care for a disappointed atheist. By doing all this, He would be entering the hearts of fragile human beings and those who seek to escape from themselves.

Jesus Christ even gained access to the heart of His enemies: The only distance between Him and the one who betrayed Him was a kiss, or the dipping of the bread in the very same wine cup. Judas, the man who was about to sell Him for thirty pieces of silver, did not intimidate Jesus. He broke bread and drank the wine of His new Covenant with both His loved ones and His betrayer. What a king we have! What a model to emulate in our daily lives!

Who is our idol? Who are we really following? I hope we follow Jesus and not the so-called super-star preacher. As noted, the extra attention, honor, care and wealth which are being laid at their feet, (often through manipulation or media) turns people into *nouveau riche* leaders who do not know how to deal with wealth in terms of the traditional biblical disciplines. They are lost in a sea of fame, pride and greed. Gradually and inevitably, they become corrupt and involved in scandals of all sorts.

It is my hope that the New Kind of Pentecostalism can consciously and deliberately deal with such issues and that people who are committed to it will not be afraid to speak out critically in a spirit of love and driven by their desire for institutional reformation. A friend of mine, a missionary to Russia, Michael Lee McDonald, once said: "The charismatic church has its own set of saints that we pray to. They are living saints, but they hold the same status as saints and icons in the Catholic and Orthodox churches. We believe that, if they pray for us, we will be healed, so we send them money to pay for their prayers on our behalf." This is true and very sad indeed.

May I conclude this first part with a positive directive: we need balance in our approach to spirituality, as well as in our dealings with finances. We also need to reassess how we treat our rising "stars", the "famous" men and women of God. Furthermore, we need to take a reasonable approach to the phenomenon of miracles. In general, we have to be more critical to our reports and numbers. Less exaggeration will attract more people to Christ. The people of the world are looking for genuine, true and honest believers. This alone can draw them to Christ.

In the next section of this work (Rethinking our Theology), I will be discussing some aspects of our Pentecostal Theology that seem to me to need review, critical evaluation and possibly revision. This corrective process will make Pentecostalism even more relevant to modern life than it is today. What I will be sharing in the coming chapters will not be easy. My writings may intimidate some readers, but that is not my intent. Rather, I strive to be upright in all that I write, and am absolutely not attempting to intimidate anyone. Therefore I would ask that readers keep an open mind as they proceed through the coming chapters and that they bring to the reading an earnest appreciation of the need for reformation as well as hope for change.

A **New** Kind of Pentecostalism

A **New** Kind of Pentecostalism

Rethinking our Theology

part two

A **New** Kind of Pentecostalism

Chapter Seven

Religion

We will thank God for what He has done in the past. That gives us a nice, safe feeling. We will declare what God will do in the future. That gives us a nice feeling of safe "excitement."

We will try to kill the prophet who says, "Today this scripture is fulfilled." The now demands faith and obedience and that is spelled "risk." Obedience now does not make us feel nice.

Stephan W. Hill[1]

My friend Steve has formulated it correctly, when it comes to what unhealthy religion can do to people. In this chapter, I seek to express what religion means in the context of a new kind of Pentecostalism. I have no doubt that there are people walking outside the walls of the organized religion who love God or Jesus, but are, at the same time, very disappointed with any religion whatsoever. Almost all organized religions have many things in common. They all talk about a better world, promote love, claim to teach truth and how to lead authentically spiritual lives. However, history has revealed just the opposite. On the assumption that there is only one true religion we have seen killing and conquest in its name.

Karl Marx (1818-1883) was right to some degree, when he claimed

---

1 - Stephen W. Hill and Marilyn Hill are founders of Harvest Now. Since 2002 they have served a disciple making movement among the peoples of Central Asia. www.harvest-now.org

that religion was the "opiate of the masses." Opium is a serious drug. It intoxicates anyone who uses it and, drugs are capable of making people do the most bizarre things- things which have drastic and often fatal consequences. Unfortunately, religion can affect people in the same way. In this chapter I attempt to describe how it functions and what kind of consequences it may have when taken literary. Pentecostalism can have these sort of addictive effects if we take its teachings literally. So, a note to my readers; please be aware that I am absolutely not speaking against organized religion. Religions have wonderful aspects, and they have done great things for humanity. However, this chapter is not about that. It is about the darker side of religion and fanaticism. Later in this chapter, I describe how this darker side of religion has penetrated Pentecostalism.

Moses' intent was not to create a religion nor was Jesus attempting to establish a new one. At the time of Jesus, there were already many religions, so there was no need to invent one. What Jesus came to do is to introduce us to a different way of life and to reveal to us the Kingdom of God. When we consider the essence of God as "goodness", "kindness", "absolute love" and "peace", and when we see Jesus as God incarnate—divine goodness and love itself come to offer mankind salvation and we who choose to follow Him become the citizens of His borderless Kingdom. We ourselves then come to manifest love and goodness through His Spirit. Every time we do so, we ourselves reveal to our fellow human beings a small foretaste, a glimpse of heaven. In His Kingdom, there is room for everyone, a place for every type of human diversity. Once we have chosen Him, we all have the opportunity to become the manifestation of His love. God is absolute Goodness, Love itself! Another translation of the phrase "The Kingdom of God" is "where God reigns" or "where love has the last word." And wherever goodness, love and kindness are being practiced, there, God reigns! There His kingdom is made manifest. "Your Kingdom come on earth as it is in heaven."

It is a fact of life that religions of all types attempt to divide people from one another. They require full submission to their rules. The benefits they promise are otherwise not forthcoming. Jesus was different. He invited everyone to come on board. During His time, there was great enmity between the Jews and the Samaritans. The Jews were very exclusive and it was very seldom that their religious establishment would accept the Samaritans. Jesus changed that. We all know the parable of the Good Samaritan. In that parable, Jesus teaches us that doing good, being a neighbor after God's heart, has nothing to do with race, ethnic background or dogma. It rather has to do with being a human being made in the image of God. Another story we read in the Bible (John, 4) is that of Jesus meeting with the Samaritan woman. As a Samaritan she, too, excluded the Jews and did so by voicing her Samaritan doctrinal principles. She suggested that Jews believe a certain place, or mountain to be the place of worship, but the Samaritans did not agree. In His reply, Jesus mentioned neither of these religious geographies as would-be places of worship. Instead, He proclaimed that man shall worship God in Spirit and Truth. He did not seem to care much about the 'letter of the law' or about doctrines that divided the Jews and Samaritans. He was showing them a different alternative. An alternative that was radically different from that which the religious establishment of the time offered.

The Lord's Prayer is another example. Just imagine Jesus with His disciples from Galilee, His disciples from a city in Samaria all together with the Pharisees from Judea. It was in this setting that He taught them how to pray. He claimed that, when they prayed, they should say "our Father"—not "my", but "our Father." In other words this God is not exclusively for Jews or certain Jewish denominations. From this point forward, He is the God of all who choose to follow Christ, to accept the good news that they have been liberated and to help others toward liberation as well.

All Religions Share Some Things in Common

There are certain things that all religions have in common, Pentecostalism included. Some of these elements tend to be negative and socially destructive e.g., religions often promote corruption and narrow-mindedness. They tend to cause man to become judgmental. They also make people live in guilt and fear of either past or future. Lastly, they do not focus much on the "now."

Corruption in Religion

All religions have various sets of laws, rules and regulations. If one follows them correctly, one will supposedly be rewarded. Breaking these laws will result in punishment, either here on earth or in the afterlife. However, man cannot follow all of these rules so he tries to find ways to secretly bypass them. In the Roman Catholic Church, priests are celibate, not allowed to marry. Similarly, for the nuns. However, they have to work together. Even though it has not been scientifically proven, this celibacy issue may create sexual frustrations and lead some of the clergy to live secret sexual lives–and often with tragic consequences. If this rule of celibacy were to be rescinded, a heavy burden would be lifted from their shoulders. As things now stand, lots of them are actually living a life of hypocrisy and personal corruption. They try to cover up their indecent acts because of a sense of guilt and shame. Of Pentecostalism, we can say the same thing: We often take the Biblical verses very literally when it suits our doctrinal purposes. When it does not, we take them figuratively. This, too, can result in hypocrisy and corruption. Consider the issue of sexual immorality and scandal among Pentecostals. We quite often quote Jesus saying: "But I tell you that anyone who looks at a woman lustfully has already committed adultery with her in his heart." (Matthew 5:28) Of course, these are the words of Jesus, but unwisely quoting this verse instills tremendous feelings of shame and guilt in both young and old, men and women. They can then only unwillingly look at members of the opposite sex.

Pentecostalism has not addressed the issue of sexuality properly. It often links irregularities in sexual behavior to demons and devils. This can indeed be the case, but we also have to realize that we are living in the twenty-first century. In the time of Jesus, social conditions were vastly different. Today, whether we like it or not, almost every day in the media we are confronted with nudity or some form of provocative behavior. Advertisements, midnight TV programs, highway billboards and Internet sites are all contributing to the creation of a society that is sexually active in the extreme. Unfortunately, this is a cause of great spiritual harm to mankind. Children are sexualized at a young age. Human trafficking is now one of the largest and fastest growing trades in the world. Slavery, as it relates to the sex industry, in sheer numbers has surpassed the entire slave trade of centuries ago[1].

In the midst of all this, Pentecostal pastors simply go on declaring that looking at a woman with lust is a sin. I agree with this but, with the exception of a few ministries, we do not openly discuss sexuality. Preaching such sermons in Pentecostal churches provokes and irritates people, it creates a group of believers who have issues with their sexuality and try to hide them. I still remember the sad incident of brother Ted Haggard, a prominent evangelical leader, who was a leading opponent of homosexuality. But, he himself was practicing it in secret! And then his situation was exposed. A very sad story indeed! I would argue that such tragedies can be avoided if we show some cultural sensitivity in our teachings and show some flexibility in our interpretation of the Bible.

Consider, for instance the issue of co-habitation, in Western societies. While this is basically a non-issue among non-believers and many moderate Christians, it poses a great problem for Pentecostals. Pentecostalism forbids co-habitation and judges it severely. Day by day, however, the number of co-habiting young Pentecostals is

---

1 - Ruffins, Ebonne. Rescuing girls from sex slavery. CNN, April 30, 2010.
http://edition.cnn.com/2010/LIVING/04/29/cnnheroes.koirala.nepal/index.html

growing. Some children of the pastors are living together in secret. They conceal their situations from their fellow churchgoers for fear of being persecuted, judged or condemned. But, some pastors also hide this sort of thing from friends and colleagues. And, yet, one pastor is known to have said that any child born out of such an illicit relationship is born with a curse!

Please do not misunderstand me here: I'm not promoting co-habitation whatsoever. I too am an advocate of classical marriage and the values attached to it, and I do believe that it both requires and produces a deeper commitment between the partners. On the other hand, I do believe, that, as Pentecostals we should not create a judgmental atmosphere if our young generation makes such choices. If we do this, they will be forced either to leave the church or to become hypocrites and live secret lives.

Our strict sermons will not only cause us to lose many souls, but they will also create frustrated people, who are suppressing their innermost problems, hiding them behind the mask of religion. Jesus Christ once said: "I have not come for those who are healthy, but for those who are sick, so that they may be healed." However, the most dangerous thing in our world is that those who are sick, and need help, pretend to be emotionally healthy and hide themselves in the church disguised as holy men and women of God. In reality, they need serious professional help, and, if they do not get it, the results will be catastrophic,— disastrous and shameful to Christianity, Pentecostalism in particular.

Overly Simplistic Thinking and Narrow Mindedness

Just like any other religion, or Christian denomination, Pentecostalism can often produce people who are very narrow-minded and whose thinking is overly simplistic. Even though Jesus said that the gate to eternal life was narrow, it was not His intention to create narrow-minded people. We are living in a complex world; our views cannot be simply categorized as good or evil, pro or con. Unfortunately, many Pentecostals are trapped in this dichotomy. Recently UNICEF released a heartbreaking and very scary report indicating that, in Sub-Saharan African countries, there is an increasing degree of violence against innocent children who are being accused by Pentecostal pastors of being witches. The Pentecostal pastors in these countries are often very simplistic in their view of evil and good, Satan and God. Due to lack of proper education, they believe that certain children who have symptoms of malnutrition, malady, or simply weak posture are witches. They are being accused of causing misfortunes for their families and their immediate community. Most of these kids are therefore abandoned, some terribly tortured, and some killed. This is something terrible and even dangerous to Pentecostalism since it is becoming an important force in the developing world. We need to sound an alarm bell on this issue.

Narrow-mindedness is a great problem, because it promotes judgmentalism. When we quote the Bible without any sense of love and compassion, we tend to generalize about people and situations. When I was a fanatic Pentecostal, I used to see the world in this way. Then I went through a transition. I realized that the world out there and the human situations we encounter are not by any means so clear cut. Later however, my view changed again. Now I have begun to realize that the world is full of colors, thousands of colors and I cannot judge people or situations based on my Bible verses and sermons. This helps me form more accurate judgments about people. Let me explain further. As mentioned earlier, in the West Christianity is now undergoing a huge transition. On the one hand, people are totally dissociating themselves from any form of organized religion, and on the other there are Western Pentecostals who are looking to reinvent or rediscover traditional ways of living a spiritual life. Their feelings towards such Pentecostal churches are filled with disappointment and bitterness. There was a time that I belonged to both groups. I would judge the traditional church on the basis of its hierarchical forms of leadership and issues with control. There was also a time that I longed to be a part of an organized church. I experienced both. Now, however, I have learned to deal with traditional churches individually, not with a judgmental spirit and bitter language, but rather looking at how relevant they are for the Kingdom of God as it can be manifest in society. There are some organized churches that are basically irrelevant to mankind, but many of them that are also doing much good.

On the other hand, many Christians do not belong to any organized church and they do many good works, things that positively impact their society and environment! Personally, I think we have to learn to make our "judgments" on an individual base and not generalize about people and churches or profile them based on what we, as individuals, have seen or experienced. In other words, we have to be careful lest we err in our assessment of them.

Guilt & Fear

God is love, so, in Him, there should be no guilt. But often religion creates guilt in peoples' hearts. This guilt industry has affected Pentecostalism as well. I often see people who are living a life of guilt towards God or the Holy Spirit. They always think, they did not give enough, they should have prayed harder or longer, or they did not love enough. Unfortunately, guilt theology can be very destructive to human consciousness and the human community. No doubt, you, too, have heard words like "do not touch the anointed one of God" or "you are robbing God, by not paying your tithes and offering" or "you don't love the State of Israel enough because you don't pray for the peace of Jerusalem" or "you have sinned against the Holy Spirit" or "don't become like Sapphira and Ananias who dropped dead after lying to Peter." Again, we should not commit the error of generalization and cast wrong judgments on people. We ought not to instill guilt and fear in people's hearts.

In closing, Jesus Christ does not represent a particular denomination. No, He actually does not! He is the very incarnation, the very translation, and the very image of God, who is LOVE. Anywhere this unconditional, selfless Love is being practiced, He will be there! He will manifest His being through those who practice this Love. Jesus Christ's intention was not to create another religion, but establish His Kingdom through those who choose to accept His message. Pentecostalism should not be considered a denomination or a religious entity in itself. It should rather be thought of as a movement of love, one that is free of fear and guilt! Its primary task should be to embrace and love human beings. However, we have turned Pentecostalism into a religious system like any other laden with dogma, disputes over scriptural interpretations, internal political rivalries and all forms of ego-driven competitiveness.

A **New** Kind of Pentecostalism

Chapter Eight

Denominations & Leadership

"Authoritarian leaders know how to control people through manipulation. In such a church no one is allowed to ask questions.[1]*"*

James Lee Grady

In the New Kind of Pentecostalism, no denomination is above any other; rather, we are all part of a larger community, even if we differ in our respective doctrinal backgrounds. Denominationalism has often divided the Church instead of uniting it. For centuries, denominations have fought each other, betrayed each other and claimed that they were the only ones who love and understand God. I am not against denominations as long as they can find their neighborly place within the Kingdom. They are, indeed, each other's neighbors, not each other's enemies. Still, I do not wish to suggest that they are faultless. We have to admit that every denomination had, and still has its own shortcomings and makes its own mistakes. We have to stop looking at the theologies that divide us, and start hoping and believing in the things that unite us.

The problem we face today is that denominations often ridicule each other, even engage in conflict over doctrinal disputes. The Catholics do not accept the Pentecostals and Pentecostals accuse the Catholics of Mary and idol worship. This should stop! There is no denomination on earth that can absolutely represent the Church, neither Roman Catholicism, nor Greek Orthodoxy, neither Protestantism nor Evangelicalism, neither Pentecostalism nor any of

1 - Grady, James Lee. "Breaking free from the spirit of control" Fire in My Bones (Charisma)
(11November 2009). www.charismamag.com/index.php/fire-in-my-bones/23911-breaking-free-from
-the-spirit-of-control

the Charismatic movements. None of them can grasp the absolute truth of the Church and its doctrines. We all have partial knowledge; each of us sees only a part of the truth. "For we know in part and we prophesy in part, but when the perfection comes, the imperfect disappears." (1 Corinthians 13: 9)

On the other hand, those who do not have any religious affiliation still do not have reason to act out of pride and arrogance. They, too, should respect the organized church for what it is. They may certainly continue to articulate their criticisms and think outside the box. Still, this gives them no right to look down upon the old-fashioned and sometimes dying church. Denominations of every type should be open to constructive criticism from within and attentive to the voice of those on the outside as well.

It must be admitted that there is a serious problem here: Denominations do not easily accept each other, but they are eager to be accepted by others. They argue, dispute, reject each other, and put one another on blacklists. They think that their understanding of theology is the right one and often allow little room for dialogue and change. What is ultimately more important; the life and teachings of Christ, or Christian theology as it has been developed by the churches? I want to know Christ and the power of His resurrection in immediate terms. He is not a theology or a system of doctrine! Christ Jesus is a revelation—to the whole of mankind: the revelation of love. He is beyond any denomination, institutional structure, or doctrinal dispute. As long as a person believes in the divinity of Christ Jesus (through revelation and not under duress), believes in His sacrifice for mankind and His resurrection and practices charity and neighborly love—as long as love is being expressed toward others—denominational differences matter not!

The time has come for growth and maturation of the church. It is now! We have to ask the Holy Spirit to lead us to understand that every denomination and non-denominational person, system, organization or church is part of a larger picture—the Kingdom of God.

From this point forward, a Catholic, an Orthodox Christian, an Evangelical, a member of the Church of the East, a Lutheran, a Baptist, a Methodist, traditional or moderate, conservative or progressive, and all those who love Jesus but do not belong to any organized church or denomination, etc. are all my brothers and sisters. Even if I may not agree with them on all of the issues, even though they may judge me, misunderstand me, misquote me, and even hate me, I still love them and see them as a part of the Body of Christ.

How long shall the Kingdom be divided against itself? Let us take the necessary steps toward ensuring that mutual understanding; love and respect prevail in our communities. Let us dialogue, share our experiences, even our theologies, with one another without being intimidated and threatened. Let us open our hands, open our arms and accept each other. Most of our disputes take place because of pre-existing bias, when we have already taken a stance on an issue and so approach one other with hostility in our hearts. When we change this and become willing to move forward in friendship, love and kindness, we will be able to truly listen to each other. Denominational disputes, battles and rivalry are a hindrance to evangelization. Young people are tired of this. They are more concerned with other issues such as social justice, the environment, poverty, and evangelization— reaching the world with the gospel of the Kingdom of God. In conclusion, concerning the denominations, I would concede that we will not be saved by any denomination or organized religious system, but only through Jesus Christ's love for mankind. Eternal life does not depend on our denomination, but on believing and following Christ—on the acts of love we commit in His name.

Leadership

Concerning Church Leadership (see Ch. 6) there are indeed apostles, prophets, evangelists, pastors and teachers as discussed in Ephesians (4:7). There is no doubt about the primary function of every ministry. Every leader should, by the very definition of leadership, serve instead of being served.

The difference between the Roman Catholic Church and the Pentecostal Church is that the Roman Catholics have only one Pope, and we have many! Too many to count! As far as the issue of equal treatment of men and women goes, the clergy should be called to task—and this should be done within the Church. We have to realize that we are serving a King of humility and meekness, a Lord with a servant's heart. He washed the feet of His disciples, broke bread and shared wine with His followers. He did not carry a crown of gold heavier than His own head, but chose a crown of thorns. When the men of God hide their inner struggles, their insecurities, their lack of personal discipline and their lack of self-confidence, behind luxury, power and prestige; when one man, draws the attention to himself, when masses of believers blindly put their trust and hope in one person—someone other than Jesus—it doesn't matter which church or denomination they belong to. Such a church is sick and needs healing! Often, the charisma of church leaders overrules any other aspect of the church, and the membership simply longs to see a performing preacher. When that preacher gets tired and burns out, that church is in trouble indeed.

So, I conclude that we truly need to reshape our view of religious leadership in twenty-first century. It does not equate to manipulation, self-enrichment or self-empowerment. It should not be based on a pyramid model, but rather a circular and flat one. By this I mean that leadership should be practiced on level ground and that it is critical that we come together around a common mission and purpose—the Kingdom of God.

Leadership & Information Technology

Whether the pastors or church leaders like it or not, people are being exposed to immense amounts of new information and continually gathering new knowledge about their religions. They are beginning to see that there are other interpretations of the Bible and other ways of practicing Christianity; they are also being exposed to heretofore untold aspects of the history of the Christian faith. Certainly, these issues bring forth reactions from the mainstream leadership, especially within the Pentecostal churches. Leaders feel threatened and insecure of their positions—a human reaction and certainly understandable. However, the question is how are we going to deal with it? Are we going to batten down the hatches, tighten up our rules and regulations, and define church structures even more rigorously? Force our people to follow the dictates of the system more exactly? Or, are we going to be open-minded and become more flexible and participate in the vast process of change that the body of Christ is now undergoing?

As a Pentecostal pastor, I see the interest in, and necessity for interacting with people by means of digital dialogue i.e. for exchanging information and allowing people under my "care" to be aware of the other side of every story. As noted above, I have chosen to redefine "church" and expand the walls of my ministry/church by adding a digital channel. And, by 'digital,' I do not mean just a website. No! What I mean is that I wish to use the capabilities of the Internet to dialogue with people, to share ideas and allow them to do the same. For instance, I choose to participate in electronic forums and discussions, but at the same time, refuse to be threatened by new ideas or new interpretations of the Bible. Instead, I dare to engage in open dialogue and discussion in the context of mutual love and respect in keeping with the message of Christ. Since I choose to do this, it might seem that I might sometimes scare people away from the church. Not so. Instead, I invite them to share their ideas with me at the table of brotherhood and "digitalhood."

A **New** Kind of Pentecostalism

Chapter Nine

The Holy Spirit

Breathe in me, O Holy Spirit, that my thoughts may all be holy.
Act in me, O Holy Spirit, that my work, too, may be holy.
Draw my heart, O Holy Spirit, that I love but what is holy.
Strengthen me, O Holy Spirit, to defend all that is holy.
Guard me, then, O Holy Spirit, that I always may be holy.
Amen.

Saint Augustine

It would be hard to find a topic in Pentecostalism that has played as central a role as that of the Holy Spirit. Similarly, it would be difficult to find one that has caused more debate between Pentecostalism and other branches of Christianity. Certain fundamental questions surround this, e.g., who is the Holy Spirit? What are the signs of being filled with the Holy Spirit? Or, being baptized in the Holy Spirit? From the time of the Azusa Street Revival[1] in 1906 until today, there have been various discussions as to what really indicates that one is filled with the Spirit. One thing is, however, undeniable: The Holy Spirit plays a crucial role in Pentecostalism.

This chapter will focus on several questions. They are less concerned with foundational theology and more with our attitudes towards the Holy Spirit and the use of His name within our religious

---

1 - The Azusa Street Revival was an historic Pentecostal revival meeting. It took place in Los Angeles, California, and was led by William J. Seymour, an African American preacher. It began with a meeting on April 14, 1906, and continued until roughly 1915. The revival was characterized by ecstatic spiritual experiences and people speaking in tongues; it also included dramatic worship services, and inter-racial mingling. Participants were criticized by both the secular media and Christian theologians for their behaviors. They were considered to be outrageous and unorthodox, especially at the time. Today, historians view this event as the primary catalyst for the spread of Pentecostalism in the twentieth century (Wikipedia).

communities. As current day Pentecostals, we have to realize that the Holy Spirit is neither our exclusive trademark of our denomination, nor limited to it! He can move anywhere and in any way He so chooses! Pneumacentrism is when we try to assess the experience of others based on our own and then try to make of it a universal standard. What are the indications of this?

First of all Pneumacentrism attempts to exclude other Christians when it comes to experiencing and having a direct relationship with the Holy Spirit. Have you ever been in meetings where the Pentecostal preacher ridicules other denominations for their lack of 'Holy Spirit power'? In fact I was once one of those who did such shameful things. I am also aware that people from other denominations may ridicule us as Pentecostals, call us names and even brand us as heretics, or spiritists. Still, we should not retaliate, not answer evil with evil, but with love! This exclusivity syndrome can create a serious problem within the universal body of Christ; it may cause others to believe that Pentecostals are narrow-minded and arrogant individuals who do not realize that the Holy Spirit can move in other denominations as well. Each of the Christian denominations speaks about and acknowledges the power of the Holy Spirit. What is it then that makes us Pentecostals think otherwise? I believe the answer may lie in how we as Pentecostals view experiencing the Holy Spirit. Often we think that this means feeling chills, falling onto the floor or speaking in tongues. This can be very beautiful; however every person has his own way of experiencing things.

Another sign of Pneumacentrism within the Pentecostal movement is noise and the belief that the noisier one gets, the more Spirit-filled one is! But this foolish assumption has caused many problems, not only in inter-denominational relationships, but also in relations between members of the Pentecostal churches. Pentecostals often criticize the non- Pentecostal denominations that they lack the direct experience of the Holy Spirit, because they are too silent and show no vitality. Let us recall the story of Elijah as he waited for God to speak to him. God did not speak in the noise of the wind, in the violence of the earthquake, or in the fire. He spoke in a soft whisper:

"The LORD said, "Go out and stand on the mountain in the presence of the LORD, for the LORD is about to pass by." Then a great and powerful wind tore the mountains apart and shattered the rocks before the LORD, but the LORD was not in the wind. After the wind there was an earthquake, but the LORD was not in the earthquake. After the earthquake came a fire, but the LORD was not in the fire. And after the fire came a gentle whisper. When Elijah heard it, he pulled his cloak over his face and went out and stood at the mouth of the cave.

1 Kings 19:11-13

As Pentecostals, we are all aware that we often use the words 'wind', 'shaking', and "fire" in our church services or conferences. We all love to see the fire of God, to experience the wind of revival and the shaking power of the Holy Spirit. In the case of Elijah, however, God did not speak to him in any of these ways. Of course God was present in all of them, for He caused them all to pass before the eyes of Elijah, but, still, He did not speak except in a whisper within Elijah's very being. Of course, the Holy Spirit can and always will manifest Himself in the form of fire, wind and a powerful shaking effect. However, when He speaks, He speaks in a gentle voice. He addresses our deepest being and speaks to our consciousness where no man can reach; no one can see or hear what is going on inside us. It is there that He addresses us quietly and gently.

Pneumacentrism can even become more hurtful and spiritually confusing, where prophecy is concerned. Listeners have to basically take it or leave it and if they leave it, there may be fatal consequences. So, I would argue that we need to reform the way we use the name of the Holy Spirit. No doubt, many of you have experienced this kind of: "Thus says the Lord" or "The Holy Spirit told me." Such words need to be carefully weighed before one utters them. They may influence other people's lives in a drastic way. We have to exercise caution in this. Unfortunately, poor communication is sometimes a problem among Pentecostals. One of the reasons for this is that, when we do not know what to say to defend ourselves, we simply use the Holy Spirit as means of escape. But, when we say things like "the Holy Spirit told me to do it" we actually close off every possible alternative or process of questioning. Doubt becomes unacceptable for most of us.

Lastly we have to ask ourselves what is genuinely a sign of being filled with, or baptized in the Holy Spirit. Most of us would likely answer: "speaking in tongues" or glossolalia. This is based on the traditional claim that, when the disciples were filled with the Holy Spirit, they all supposedly spoke in tongues (Book of Acts, 2). Speaking in tongues has unfortunately become the trademark for Pentecostalism. But, on the other hand, many of us misuse this gift and some even despise other Christian denominations that do not practice it. I however, do not believe that speaking in tongues is the only sign of being filled with Holy Spirit! For me the real indication of this is the unconditional, boundless love that the Holy Spirit pours into our hearts. As the apostle Paul writes:

> *"If I speak in the tongues of men and of angels, but have not love, I am only a resounding gong or a clanging cymbal. If I have the gift of prophecy and can fathom all mysteries and all knowledge, and if I have a faith that can move mountains, but have not love, I am nothing. If I give all I possess to the poor and surrender my body to the flames, but have not love, I gain nothing."*
>
> 1 Corinthians 13:1-3

Notice that he states explicitly, that, if he speaks in tongues of men and angels but has no love, he is nothing! Love is a power. Love it is a force. Love is the most powerful positive force since it has the power to prevent atrocities, undermine prejudices, build bridges, and bind us together. In the Book of Acts (1), Jesus Christ requests that the disciples not leave Jerusalem but wait until the Holy Spirit comes upon them. It is then that they shall receive true spiritual power. He said to them:

"It is not for you to know the times or dates the Father has set by his own authority. 8 But you will receive power when the Holy Spirit comes on you; and you will be my witnesses in Jerusalem, and in all Judea and Samaria, and to the ends of the earth."

Acts 1:7-8

As a Pentecostal, I have always believed that this power Jesus spoke about is the power of signs and wonders that I often see on Christian cable TV. It causes people to fall down on the floor when I pray for them; similarly, when I prophesy, signs and wonders follow and people stand in amazement! Of course all of these things can be signs and manifestations of the Holy Spirit, but, as I grew in the Lord, I realized that the power Jesus spoke about is that of love. The experience of unconditional love makes us do things that we were incapable of doing. Love moves us to serve people that we were unable to love, to go places we were unable to go and do the hardest jobs. Mother Theresa did what she did for the sake of people and in the name of her Lord Jesus Christ. Her work can only have been inspired by unconditional love. It was the Holy Spirit that moved Martin Luther King to advocate for abolition of the racist blindness that dominated in the United States in his time. It was the Holy Spirit that gave him the courage to face the possibility of becoming a martyr for Justice. Roger E. Olson, a former member of the Pentecostal movement, who teaches at George W. Truett Theological Seminary at Baylor University in Waco, Texas, writes the following:

> *Billy Graham was and is a great hero to most Pentecostals, but he says he has never spoken in tongues. Is he not Spirit-filled? My questions on this issue were deftly turned aside, and subtle aspersions were cast on my spirituality merely for asking such questions. In the end, I was told that Graham is fully Spirit-filled even if he has never spoken in tongues. He's the one exception. But were I to take up a career teaching theology in a Pentecostal college (I was told), I couldn't teach that there might be exceptions to that distinctive doctrine. The cognitive dissonance wrought by this and other answers boggled my mind.[1]*

Love is as sweet as honey for those who love goodness and light, but is bitter and has great destructive force for to those who hate goodness and enjoy darkness. Love is the sign of the Holy Spirit. I once said that when a person risks his or her life for the sake of Jesus and for the love of his or her fellow humans, when someone goes to the most dangerous areas in the world to distribute medicine for the poor, he or she is as much filled with Holy Spirit as the one who is praying in tongues in a fully air-conditioned church in the affluent West! Unfortunately, we have hurt many through the arrogance and inflated self-confidence we derive from praying in tongues. We have to embrace all of our other Christian brothers and sisters. It can be that their expression of the Holy Spirit, or their experience is different than ours, but they still know Him and His power. What binds us here is the love that He pours in our hearts: Love is a force, a vast and almost untamable power, or as the Greeks said it, "dunamis."

1 - Olson, Roger E. Pentecostalism's Dark Side. (Article) www.religion-online.org/showarticle.asp?title=3338

Chapter Ten

The Holy Bible

In the beginning was the Word, and the Word was with God,
and the Word was God. He was with God in the beginning.
Through him all things were made; without him nothing
was made that has been made.

John 1:1-3

There have been ongoing discussions about the Bible and its role in Christianity, and, of course, in Pentecostalism in particular. In this connection, one question needs to be asked: What exactly is the Word of God? Many people have pondered this. Some take the Bible to be the infallible Word of God, others believe that the Word of God is Jesus Himself. I would argue that we have to find a balance between these two extremes: Jesus Christ is the ultimate, absolute Word of God. His life, His being and the ultimate Word:

In the beginning was the Word, and the Word was with God,
and the Word was God. He was with God in the beginning.
Through him all things were made; without him nothing was
made that has been made. In him was life, and that life was the
light of all mankind. The light shines in the darkness, and the
darkness has not overcome it.

John 1:5

On the other hand, if this is the case, then what is the Holy Bible? I believe the Bible to have been inspired by the Holy Spirit. But it is also the word of God as recorded by man. I therefore call the Bible, the Holy Scripture. Therefore, the Bible should be read and understood from the perspective of the life of Christ Jesus and interpreted on the basis of the principles He taught.

Multiple systematic mistakes are committed when it comes to dealing with the Bible. First of all, many Pentecostals use different measures when reading it. We draw only on certain segments of it. For instance, when it comes to tithes and offerings, we quote the Bible and literally believe that paying the tithes and offering as written in the book Malachi will bring a blessing to the donor. Of course, this can be true, but if a person does not give, some of us preach that they will be cursed. On the other hand, when it comes to other rules or biblical verses, we interpret them more broadly. Circumcision is a case in point. I do not think that the vast majority of the Pentecostals in the west would consider being circumcised as a condition of becoming a Christian. But, in my view, this creates a kind of unconscious hypocrisy. It amounts to following the Bible based on a double standard. What will the consequences be if we force our biblical interpretations on other people?

No one has the right to force his/her interpretation of the Bible on someone else as long as we all agree on the basic foundations of our faith: Jesus is the way to salvation in so far as He died and was resurrected, and this, together with the guidelines for living a consecrated life as they are described in the Bible. All who believe in Him will be saved. Since we live in a time of God's Grace, it is clear that we do not live under the curse or conditions of bondage of the Old Testament. The coming of Jesus Christ to the world has brought Grace to mankind.

Secondly, when it comes to Biblical interpretation and theology, it seems to me that in Pentecostalism, we often tend to solve our theological problems by drawing primarily on the thought of Paul, the apostle. We even read the Bible from his spiritual perspective, not from that of Christ Himself. Consider the following example: In Christianity, many discuss the role of women in the ministry. If we take the advice of Paul entirely literally, I would have to admit, unfortunately, that women can have no place in the ministry. Or, if we take the Old Testament as a guide in this, the role of the woman is also not clear, especially when it comes to ministry. To decide a question like this, I ought rather to go directly to Jesus.

The Gospels reveal how He treated women. His sayings and His actions lead us to conclude that He was very revolutionary when it comes to the question of the role of the woman not only in the ministry, but also in society as a whole. He traveled with them and even associated with prostitutes and adulterers. I cannot take what Paul says about women as the criterion for deciding this issue, nor can I refer to the Old Testament. Instead, as a Pentecostal, I turn directly to Jesus Christ—and, at the same time, seek advice from the Holy Spirit. That is, I try to find my answers in the gospels as well as my own powers of common sense, and listen to the subtle whisper of God's voice within my heart. Having done these things, I would also place my decision in the context of the time in which we live. St. Paul's time is clearly past, nor is it the case that he lives in our time. Therefore, I conclude that women do indeed have an important place in the ministry. But, this is only one issue.

Those who take a literal approach to reading the Bible often turn out to be very judgmental, to have less feeling for real life matters, to be very dogmatic and simplistic in their thinking. On the other hand, those who read scripture selectively in order to defend or justify their positions can sometimes be hypocritical. In contrast to both of these, those who choose Jesus as their Savior, honor Him as the Word of God, take Him as a model for their lives and, at the same time, give thorough consideration to Biblical verses will, in the end, be more considerate of others, sensitive to their struggles, less judgmental and overall more loving and compassionate.

If we simply use the Bible to prove right and wrong and behave judgmentally, if we take it to be exclusively the Word of God, then perhaps we are engaging in a form of idolatry. Who do we love more, Jesus or the Bible? Of course, I do love the Bible, but I will not always choose to live precisely in keeping with its dictates. If I did, then I would have to condone things like stoning people to death for adultery. We still often follow the "eye–for-an-eye" system of justice, and we still think we have the right to conquer other nations, tribes and peoples, even commit genocide because all of these can be found in the Bible. However, one can also find there the life story and spiritual teachings of the Lord of Lords, Jesus Christ, the compassionate, the merciful, the very incarnation of love! I do not need Solomon's wisdom or David's forms of worship, but rather the Wisdom of Jesus Christ. I need the experience of prayer and worship, of being the living sacrifice for His sake. So, when I read the Bible, I read it only through the eyes of Jesus Christ. It is thus that I can allow the Holy Spirit to guide me in my decisions.

Interpretation of scriptures depends not only on historical context, as some theologians suggest. It is also not only transmitted from God through the Holy Spirit to the individual, but much of our understanding of it depends on the nature of our own times. Seven hundred years ago, the Roman Catholic Church believed that the earth was flat simply because it had not been shown to be otherwise! Their view was based on literary interpretations of the scriptures: The Bible spoke about the "ends of the earth," or the "four corners of the earth." Of course, those who genuinely believed this were equally as sincerely committed to Christianity as some of us are today. However, things changed when scientists discovered the curvature of the globe. To the Church, this was an abomination, a defilement of established belief, so they persecuted those who proclaimed it.

Another issue relating to Biblical interpretation can be our understanding of our time as the end time. The idea of the end time has produced a most intriguing discussion among Christians, especially Pentecostals.

Sometimes it seems that the Pentecostal movement overemphasizes this—and in a really flashy way! There is no doubt that the Pentecostal movement is interested in helping people get into heaven, but it should also focus on the now. People are suffering in the here and now! Creation languishes under the burden of its own darkness and ignorance! God wants to use us as instruments of love and peace, and reconciliation between ourselves and Him and between nature and man!

When the end time claims mix with the political interests of countries and nations around the world, then all of this becomes even more dangerous. I do believe in the end times, but I do not want to offer a prognosis on this–only the Father knows the time and the hour.

"But about that day or hour no one knows, not even the angels in heaven, nor the Son, but only the Father."

Matthew 24:36

Unfortunately, we are currently experiencing a commercialized form of eschatology, one that deals in good and evil. Most of the time it fits with the national interests of Western countries, particularly when non-Western nations are often compared to the anti-Christ. Since the events of 9/11 and throughout the first decade of the new millennium, tensions between the West and Islam have escalated. Things like the Iranian ambition for membership in the nuclear club have stimulated the commercialization of end time theories. Where eschatology is concerned, books, DVDs and other materials are now being sold like never before.

Respect for a diversity of opinions is essential, but I tend to disagree with the way this kind of eschatological interpretation of our times has come to dominate our thinking. All of these various publications are but interpretations of our world situation. Not a single one of them can prove that his/her thinking about this is correct.

The tensions between West and East—and also North and South—bring me to my next point. It too concerns the Bible and how it is interpreted.

The Bible: A Matter of East and West

Another important point about the Bible is the question of how we view it. Is it a book that represents Western civilization, or a book of the East? Ought we to read it through the eyes of Socrates and Plato i.e. from the perspective of Hellenistic culture? Or do we have to return to the East, to Israel and Palestine to understand it? Are Greek and Latin more important than Hebrew and Aramaic? Of course, all of them are important, but the West has overemphasized the former. Somehow Western Christianity does not give so much attention to Hebrew, and even less to Aramaic. This fact has piqued my interest in Aramaic, the language of Jesus. In studying it, I have come upon some interesting and amazing information that will challenge many of our current theological and biblical interpretations. The West and the East have always been in dialogue, yet also in conflict as far as their way of thinking is concerned. Western culture and theology are rooted in certain dualistic assumptions about reality: the distinction between good or evil, the spiritual and the carnal, etc. In contrast to this, Easterners do not view the world as dichotomous. Scholars of the Church of the East, such as the Assyrians, suggest that a great part of the New Testament was probably not initially written in Greek, but originally in Aramaic, the language spoken by Jesus and all His disciples (with the exception of Judas Iscariot). Indeed, all of them spoke Aramaic and Hebrew. To support this assertion, these scholars suggest that a fisherman like Peter could not speak or write Greek. He most likely wrote or dictated his letters in Aramaic and they were then later translated into Greek. This is also thought to be the case for the gospels. During the process of translation from Aramaic to Greek, the translators may have made unconscious mistakes, and these errors then persist in the modern day translations of the Bible. No doubt, the information I am about to share will seem very challenging to many, but I find it worthwhile to do so. It may even solve some age-old questions about certain biblical texts.

The Aramaic Language

During the time of Jesus Christ, various Aramaic dialects were spoken in the region of Palestine; one of these dialects was Northern Galilean, while another was Chaldean Aramaic, a dialect spoken in the Southern region. In 722 BC, the ten tribes of Israel were carried into captivity in Babylon. Their land was given to the Assyrians who had been brought to Palestine from other parts of the Middle East, such as regions beyond the Euphrates. The Hebrew language was therefore gradually transformed into Aramaic. Even today, many Jews in Kurdistan speak a language called Leshan Galosh, the language of captivity, which is the same as Northern Aramaic—the language that Jesus spoke. The Jews in southern Israel or Judea, and also those in Persia, spoke Southern Aramaic, better known as Chaldean.

Many differences can be identified between the Aramaic that Jesus spoke and the Chaldean language. The Galileans often spoke in metaphors and parables and these were often rendered literally. This caused confusion and obscured, or sometimes entirely erased original meanings. Also, we must keep in mind that words often have double and even triple meanings in Aramaic, especially northern Aramaic. Many of these words with multiple meanings were also mistranslated into Greek and later into English. In what follows, I discuss some of these words and verses from the Bible. Another consideration here is that some interpretations of the Biblical verses from the New Testament should actually be worked out in keeping with our knowledge of Aramaic and Jewish customs, not on the assumption that Greco-Roman culture was the locus of the events of the New Testament.

The Lord's Prayer

"Lead us not into temptation, but deliver us from evil . . ."

Matthew 6:13 NIV

The meaning of this phrase in the original Aramaic language is "prevent us (part us) from making a mistake" or "do not let us or allow us to enter into temptation." In other words, God does not lead anyone into temptation. In fact, it is Satan who tempts. In James 1:13, we read that "God cannot be tempted nor does He tempt anyone" (NIV). In Aramaic, the word patzan means "part us from evil" and not "deliver us" from evil[1] (Lamsa, 1999).

The Camel and the Needle

"It is easier for a camel to go through the eye of a needle,   than for a rich man to enter into the kingdom of God."

Matthew 19:24 KJV

In Aramaic, the word gamla has three different meanings depending on its pronunciation. Although it is written in the same way, it is pronounced differently to produce different meanings. This is something that would have been learned in the culture from childhood. Based on the context a reader would know the proper pronunciation. This is true for many Middle Eastern languages, including Persian and Arabic.

What does gamla mean? It can mean a camel, but also it can also mean a large rope! In this case, it means a large or thick rope, not a camel. Of course, alternative explanations of this verse have been suggested in Western theological circles: The hole or gate in the wall of Jerusalem was called the 'eye of the needle.' However, no

---

1 - Lamsa, George, Gospel Light: A Revised Annotated Edition. Covington, GA:
The Aramaic Bible Society, 1999.
2 - Roth, Andrew Gabriel, Ruach Qadim: Aramaic Origins of the New Testament.
Lexington, KY: Tushiyah Press, 2009.

historically or archeologically proven evidence has been produced in support of this. Thus, if rendered literally from the Aramaic, Matthew 19:24 means: "It is easier for a rope to go through the eye of a needle than for a rich man to enter into the Kingdom of God.[2]"

My God, My God why have you forsaken me?

"And about the ninth hour Jesus cried with a loud voice saying, Eli, Eli, lama sabachtani. That is to say, my God, my God, why have you forsaken me? Some of them that stood there, when they heard that, said, this man calls for Elias."

Matthew 27:46-47 AKJV

This is another example of a fatal mistake in translation of the original text. First of all, why would people in Jerusalem have thought that Jesus was calling Elias? If they spoke in traditional Hebrew, they would have known that Eli does not mean Elias!

In other words, Eli, Eli, Lama Sabachtani was not spoken in Hebrew, but in Northern Aramaic or Galilean. Indeed, we read in the Gospels that Jesus often used Aramaic words. Putting these facts together, what does Eli, Eli, Lama Sabachtani then mean?

The Aramaic word 'Shbaqthani' is rooted in the word shbaq, which means "to keep," "to preserve," "to spare," and also "to forgive," or "to allow." The last letter of the word Shbaqthani indicates that this is the first person singular form of the verb. Therefore in Aramaic, Eli, Eli, Lama Sabachtani means "My God, My God, for this I was sent."

In other words, if we freely translate this verse from the original language, it means, "My God, My God, for a time such as this I was kept" or "For this purpose I was kept"[3].

---

3 - Lamsa, George, Gospel Light: A revised Annotated Edition. Covington, GA: The Aramaic Bible Society, 1999.

Sweat turned into blood

"And being in an agony he prayed more earnestly, and his sweat was as it were great drops of blood . . . "

Luke 22:44 KJV

In the northern Aramaic language, an oft quoted saying is "sweat turning into blood," meaning that someone is suffering or in agony. Thus, in the original this passage would not mean that he literally sweated. The phrase is more likely intended to be understood metaphorically.

Peter the Rock

"[Jesus] said: 'You are Simon the son of Jona; you shall be called Cephas, which is by interpretation, a stone.'"

John 1:42 AKJV

In the Middle East, especially in the context of the Northern Galilean dialect, people tend to call each other by nicknames that suit their character. Jesus Called Simon by the Aramaic name "Kepa", which means stone. Peter did not grasp things easily and could not quickly understand information. So the name 'Stone' would mean something like our expression "hard headed."

We have to imagine what happened when Peter finally grasped who Jesus was, namely the Messiah, the Son of God. We often believe that Jesus meant that upon this "Stone," i.e., this "rock," He would build His church. It actually means that even this Stone (i.e., Peter, the one who does not grasp spiritual ideas easily) eventually got it, and upon this revelation, the Lord will build His church.

The Wedding Feast at Cana

"And when they wanted wine, the mother of Jesus said unto him, 'They have no wine.' Jesus said unto her, 'Woman what have I to do with you? My hour is not yet come.'"

John 2:3-4 AKJV

According to Dr. Lamsa, this verse should read as follows if it is to be translated accurately from the original Aramaic: "What is it to me and to you, woman? My turn has not come yet." The Aramaic word "shaa" means "hour," "time," and "turn." The original translators apparently made errors both in the translation and the interpretation of the wedding custom. In those days, and even today in some places in the Middle East, custom dictates that during a wedding ceremony, the men sit on the floor according to their rank and position. The bridegroom offers the food, but the wine is bought or purchased in turns by those men who are sitting in line.

They may request more wine from the servants. In this context, one would understand that Jesus did not mean that His time to carry out His ministry had not yet come, but rather that His turn to simply buy the wine had not.[4]

Moreover, in the Galilean / Jewish custom, the priests normally did not order wine because they believed that excess drinking could cause fights to break out. They generally requested water instead. Here we can see the divine wisdom of Jesus Christ as high priest. He did not break the custom, but instead ordered water to be brought in. Yet, the water miraculously turned into wine. Just like in the story of John 8, where an adulterous woman was brought to Jesus in order to test him, Jesus wisely did not break the law and yet simultaneously offered grace.

At the wedding feast of Cana, He did not break with the custom by requesting water, yet offered the best wine for the guests.

---

4 -Lamsa, George, Gospel Light: A revised Annotated Edition. Covington, GA: The Aramaic Bible Society, 1999.

Eating Jesus Flesh & Blood?

"Jesus said unto them, 'Verily, verily, I say unto you, except ye eat the flesh of the Son of man, and drink his blood, ye have no life in you."

John 6:53 KJV

This is also a very interesting verse for analysis. As John 6 states, after Jesus said this, many who had followed Him left at this point. Why? They did not really understand His words; even some Jews did not comprehend the Northern Galilean dialect. According to Dr. Lamsa, it contains the following saying: "I have eaten my body and drunk my blood" (Lamsa, 1999). This means that the speaker has worked hard and suffered even to the point of dying. Therefore, by incorporating this saying into His teaching, i.e., "eating His blood and His body," Jesus meant that His followers should be ready to suffer even to the point of death for the sake of the Gospel and Christ's message, just like Jesus Himself was called to do.

A literal translation of this verse can cause a misunderstanding. During the early period of persecution of the church (100–200 AD) Christians were, for example, wrongly accused of cannibalism.

Hating your father and mother?

"If anyone comes to me and does not hate his father and mother, his wife and children, his brothers and sisters—yes, even his own life—he cannot be my disciple." - emphasis added

Luke 14:26 NIV

In Aramaic, the word for "hate" has a dual meaning. It can mean indeed 'hate,' but it can also mean "put aside." Context dictates how it is to be rendered.

In Aramaic, this passage literally means, "He who cannot put aside his father, mother . . . even his life cannot be my disciple." How many times have young Christians hurt their parents and family members as a result of their misunderstanding this verse? Jesus clearly never asked us to hate anyone.

Do not call anyone Teacher

Jesus said "Nor are you to be called 'teacher,' for you have one Teacher, the Christ."

Matthew 23:10 NIV

This verse is oft misconstrued. Sometimes I meet Christians who tell me that they do not need any one to teach them because Jesus said to not call anyone teacher. If that is true, why did the very same Jesus command His disciples to go and teach the world what He had taught them? The error here is in the translation and it derives from a lack of knowledge of the Aramaic.

Also, the Aramaic word for teacher is Rabbi. But, this word has a double meaning; the first is "teacher," the second, "my great one" or "my exalted one." i.e. "Rab" means "great," and "I" means "my." So, when Jesus instructed His disciples and listeners to not call any one Rabbi, He meant "Do not exalt any one, or do not call any one 'my great one'"[5].

In closing, I would note that my intention here is not simply to point up errors or mistranslations, but rather to create a space for dialogue between East and West, and even North and South where biblical interpretation is concerned. By no means do I wish to suggest that the Eastern interpretation is the correct one, not at all! Nevertheless, I do believe that East and West can learn a great deal from each other on such questions.

---

5 - Roth, Andrew Gabriel, Ruach Qadim: Aramaic Origins of the New Testament. Lexington, KY Tushiyah Press, 2009

We often castigate as heretics people whose views are different than ours. Mass ignorance is one of the greatest problems of our time. People who think differently than we do are easily called names, put into boxes with the labels of our own creation. I truly hope that the traditional Western theological education will give an increasing amount of attention to the cultural, historic and linguistic aspects of the Aramaic language. If we want to understand the message of Jesus Christ, we have to enlarge our knowledge of both Aramaic, the language He spoke, and the Judaic culture in which He lived.

A **New** Kind of Pentecostalism

A **New** Kind of Pentecostalism

Promoting **Change**

part three

A **New** Kind of Pentecostalism

Chapter Eleven

Dialogue with the Other

You cannot paint white on white or black on black.
Everyone needs the Other in order to be seen.

Manu Dibango[1]

If we desire positive change and seek to participate in the process of bringing it about, we have to promote dialogue. Dialogue is better than war and also better than dispute. Dialogue gives us the opportunity to learn from others. In the context of this New Kind of Pentecostalism, I suggest that it ought to take on various dimensions: dialogue with science, dialogue with cultures and dialogue with other religions, especially Islam. This chapter will address the first two. I discuss dialogue with Islam separately in a later chapter. People who love to dialogue are bridge builders. But they are often misunderstood by both of the sides they are attempting to connect.

What do I mean by dialogue? Conversation, mutual exchange of knowledge, information, and opinion while respecting the other without losing one's own sense of identity. Dialogue means to put aside any tendency to take offence, learning to listen carefully and also learning to criticize gracefully. It is an enriching interchange between peoples, religions and cultures. Oftentimes, we can find "truth" in the words of our opponents; somehow they are our mirrors. They show us our flaws and shortcomings. Someone who doesn't like to face reality is always running away from the "mirror." I

---

1 - Manu Dibango is one of Africa's most famous saxophonists in Europe. He was born in Cameroon in 1933.
He is a leading personality in African music. Dibango has also been an active journalist, ethnologist and philosopher.

remember when I weighed almost one hundred kilograms—heavily overweight—I used to avoid looking into any sort of mirror, because I knew what I would see. But, now that I have lost more than twenty kilograms, I am able to face myself again. When I was heavier, I avoided doing this because I was not at peace with myself. Yet, I would blame the mirror! Those who lack self-confidence, those who are not satisfied with themselves are those who break the "mirrors", and who also avoid "others." Moreover, they are people who prefer war instead of dialogue! Pentecost is fundamentally about fellowship and dialogue! As long as I cannot sit at the table of brotherhood/sisterhood and eat, drink, talk and share with you, I cannot practice my faith in fullness. I only can live in freedom, when my neighbor does; I am only loved, when my neighbor is; I am only blessed when my neighbor is! Therefore I have to love just as Christ does. This is the true sense of Pentecost!

Science, other cultures, religions, and even atheism can be the best mirrors. They can remind us of the things we have neglected or somehow failed to address. They can overwhelm us with questions we have either run from or long ignored. Lastly, as Pentecostals, we can choose either to war with them or open a dialogue. Yes, even something this serious is a matter of human choice.

Dialogue with Science

In Western culture, science and religion became separated from each other in the Middle Ages. The shortsightedness of the religious establishment of that time drove the scientists out of the Church. Many of them were persecuted, some even killed, because of their scientific discoveries, e.g., the curvature of the earth, the movement of the sun around the earth and many other things. The Church has long been too hostile to science and, conversely, science has all too readily trivialized religion. We have to admit that there are some matters that neither the Bible nor Christian revelation can explain; however, they can be explained by science.

Science can even help us in our evangelical efforts. Uchimura Kanzo (1861-1930), a prominent Japanese Christian thinker and the founder of Non-Church Movement[2] (1901), believed that "since one cannot serve God without serving people, the purpose of evangelism is for the people and to relieve the world from suffering." To become qualified evangelists one must have not only knowledge of the Bible but knowledge of history (including sociology), and science as well. An evangelist will be even more effective when he has knowledge in other areas such as agriculture, biology and economy. Kanzo believed that "if evangelists had only theological knowledge, they could teach divinity students, but not guide and help carpenters, farmers, merchants, scholars and politicians."[3] If we want to understand God, we not only have to read the Bible and have a personal relation with Jesus Christ, but also see the mind of God in nature and in all of creation. If, as believers, we agree that God created the heavens and the earth, then the mind and thought pattern of God can be discerned even in the molecule or in an individual cell, in a single leaf, or in the system of nature itself, including the stars and galaxies. In all things, we can find evidence of God. Therefore studying science and understanding nature, indeed, learning any kind of science, is bound to bring us closer to Him and bridge the gap between the divine and us. Most of Christ's parables were taken from nature. He spoke, for example, of trees, seeds, sparrows and mountains.

The natural sciences inspire me to understand the mind of God. The social sciences help me to understand my fellow humans whom God has urged me to love and care for. History, as science, teaches me to learn from the mistakes of the past, and theology helps me to relate all these sciences to Almighty God, who redeemed mankind through Jesus Christ. But, the list goes on and on. The Church should lend an ear to ideas and theories that are not widely agreed upon within

---

2 - The Non-Church Movement, or Mukyukai: Uchimura Kanzo did not believe in the organized religion. Instead, He believed in a non-institutionalized, independent and a free church. For his church was not a building but fellowship of the followers of Jesus Christ. This movement was and still is very popular in Japan.
3 - Miura, Hiroshi. The Life and Thoughts of Uchimura Kanzo 1861-1930. Wm. B. Eerdmans Publishing, 1996.

its walls. It should dialogue with those who believe in the theory of evolution and other theories as well. We do not have to agree with them, but we can at least hear them out.

Let us not repeat the mistakes of the Medieval Church. Too often we have persecuted and ex-communicated our brothers and sisters who have different scientific ideas than those of the mainstream Church—sent them into the fires of hell simply because their values are different from ours where knowledge is concerned. Yet, often these men and women still believe in Jesus. It is He who grants us salvation and our salvation does not depend on scientific views. Hard-line Pentecostals often go so far as to demonize Christians who "believe" in the theory of evolution. Christian evolutionists are being excommunicated simply because they believe in some aspect or other of the theory.

When we enter into dialogue with science, we can even read the Bible from a scientific perspective and in a way that is affirmative of our theology. As a Pentecostal, I read the Bible as a spiritual book. I consistently learn many things from it on a personal level, things that can help me to improve my personal life. On the other hand, as a sociologist I also read and interpret it in a sociological context. Combining these two is very fulfilling and enriching. Let me give you some examples.

In the Book of Genesis, for instance, we read how God created the heavens and earth and how He made man in His own image. We also learn how Adam and Eve fell into the mistake of eating from the fruit of the tree of good and evil. The serpent tempted Eve by showing her the tree of life and challenged her with the powers that are within this particular tree and its fruit. The forbidden tree was pleasant to the eyes and the temptation was great, almost impossible to resist. The result was that Eve felt entrapped by the Serpent. As someone who loves to analyze society, I can here comment on the power of advertisement in our capitalistic world. The advertising industry oftentimes deceives consumers; it sells things on the basis of lies, either outright or subtle. Some things are just too good to be true: Coca-Cola can never bring peace to the world and when you use a certain cream, your seventy year-old skin will not turn into the skin of a thirty year old. The result of all of this deception is terrible: People become compulsive shoppers. They buy more and more the things that they actually have no need of—a circumstance that can only eventually lead to their financial demise.

Reading the story of Cain and Abel reminds me of what we learn at school. Human history goes through stages, and human beings were once upon a time hunters-gatherers, not bound to a specific territory. As they hunted or ate from the trees, they would roam around and discover new territories. Gradually these people discovered cultivation and farming. Many of them came to settle in a specific area and territories were defined. On the other hand, the number of hunter-gatherers was declining. The oldest wars in human history can be traced back to migration patterns of these nomads and the more settled groups. Cain is a sort of settler and Abel is the landless hunter-gatherer. Cain killed Abel, just like the settlers gradually killed off the hunters-gatherers. So, in my reading, Cain and Abel may have been real individuals who existed at one time, but they also represent entire groups of people and even generations. Moreover, Adam was a name of a person, and, at the same time, the name for all humanity; similarly for Israel and Jacob.

The Book of Genesis discusses the life of a very important person: Abraham. As he was about sacrifice his own son to God, the Lord substituted a ram instead of the boy. Of course, I do believe that Abraham actually existed, that he is a real historical figure, but, at the same time, I place his story in a sociological context. Some interesting facts come to light when one approaches the text in this way. Thousands of years ago, humanity not only worshipped diverse deities, but also sacrificed human beings to them, in some cases, even their own children. Later, of course, we realized that killing other human beings to propitiate the gods was not the proper way to honor them. When morality began to play a role, human beings started to sacrifice animals instead. Thus the story of Abraham fits in with the theory of social evolution. Such examples abound, and I do believe that even scientists from other disciplines such as medicine, geography, biology or mathematics can all place their work and theories within a larger theological context.

Often intellectualism is seen by Pentecostals almost as a sin. As Roger Olson writes:

> *Not all Pentecostals are anti-intellectual or revel in incoherence. But a deep antipathy to critical rationality applied to theology is a hallmark of the movement. Too often spiritual abuse in the form of shame is directed at those, especially young people, who dare to question the teachings of highly placed Pentecostal ministers and evangelists...I was one of the first Open Bible members to attend seminary and, like most Pentecostals who did that, I left the movement. I felt pushed out for wasting my time on intellectual pursuits rather than becoming a missionary or evangelist. Today evangelical seminaries are full of Pentecostal youths. Many of them still find doors closed when they return to their home denominations for ordination or for leadership positions in churches. Pentecostal scholars too often have to work outside Pentecostal institutions and live in the shadows and on the margins of the movement.*[4]

Let us not drive our intellectuals out of the church, but rather dialogue with them. I do hope that as the New Kind of Pentecostal believers we will be able to reach out to scientists and other academics start learning from them and also allow them to learn from us.

---

4 - Olson, Roger E. Pentecostalism's Dark Side. (Article). www.religion-online.org/showarticle.asp?title=3338

Dialogue with Other Cultures

Culture is defined as the sum of the ideas, beliefs, behaviors and products connected with a group or a society. In short, it is a society's way of life. Culture encompasses everything that we as humans create and everything we possess. It is based on two types of concepts: the material and the non-material. Material concepts are tangible, touchable, visible objects that are unique to a certain culture, whereas non-material ones are abstract. They consist of such things as norms, values, language, religious beliefs artistic expressions, music, and myths. One of the important aspects of Pentecostalism is the fulfillment of the Great Commission as required by Jesus Christ:

> *Then Jesus came to them and said, "All authority in heaven and on earth has been given to me. Therefore go and make disciples of all nations, baptizing them in the name of the Father and of the Son and of the Holy Spirit, and teaching them to obey everything I have commanded you. And surely I am with you always, to the very end of the age."*
>
> Matthew 28:18-20

We as Pentecostals place great value on this. In order to fulfill such a commission, we need a broader understanding of the cultures of the nations we are trying to reach with the gospel. Often Christianity has become insensitive to the reality of other cultures. Culture is a very effective door for communication and sharing the good news of Jesus Christ. Unfortunately, however, through the media, Western Pentecostalism has begun to influence Pentecostalism elsewhere. I often travel to various non-western countries for conferences, and, at almost all of them I see American / Western influences at work in their worship services. In some cultures even traditional musical instruments are considered demonic and pagan. On the other hand, non Western Christians adopt such attitudes and exercise the same type of cultural hegemony over others when they travel abroad.

Cultural sensitivity is very important if we are to reach other nations with the Gospel.

Often when Christianity is presented as the religion of the superpowers, it becomes visibly dominant. History has proved this to be the case. From the fourth century onward, it became the leading religion of the Greco-Romano world. One consequence of this was that Greek and Latin became the "language" of God, thus Hellenistic and Roman views of Christianity overruled all other forms of it. Similarly, in the fifteenth and sixteenth centuries, the rise of the Spanish and Portuguese caused Roman Catholicism to spread across the globe. Spanish/Portuguese Christianity became visibly dominant everywhere. The reformation in the sixteenth century, and its collaboration with the Western and Northern European governments, produced a reformed, Protestant theology which came to dominate certain parts of the world. For the past two hundred years or more, Anglo-American Christianity and its relationship to British and American territorial expansion have had significant consequences for the world as whole. One of these consequences is that English became the language of evangelical religion. Christianity took a commercial course and came to dominate the worship and literature industry worldwide.

Today, there is nowhere in the world where students of theology bypass American and English Christian literature and writers. Church history also means Reformation history and theology means Anglo-American Evangelical or Dutch Reformed theology. The dominance of Western Christianity throughout the world has evoked two major reactions in the non-western world: 1) Almost total acceptance and implementation of this Western Theology with minor concessions to, native cultural influences. Evangelical Christianity in the Philippines is, for example, very much American-influenced, Korean Protestantism is based on Reformed Theology, and, in Africa, American prosperity-mindedness preached from satellite TV stations inspires Pentecostalism. 2) In some cases, people have not totally surrendered to the influence of imported Christianity, but sought to develop a version of it on the basis of an indigenous theology. Unfortunately, there are relatively few countries that have been able to deal with this problem creatively. Japan, in the course of late nineteenth and early twentieth centuries, attempted this. In his work, The Japanese contribution to Christian Theology (1960), Carl Michelson indicated that even though Protestant Christianity was relatively young in Japan, it was apparently the first country that developed its own unique version of Christian theology.[5]

Uchimura Kanzo (1861-1930) believed that only a Japanese form of Christianity could save Japan. After his conversion experience and intense study of the Holy Scriptures, he was gradually confronted with a very difficult reality: the Western missionaries did not only bring Christianity to Japan, but they also brought with them their own cultures—and all of this in the name of Christianity. It became clear to him that the Christianity introduced there by Westerners carried with it a Western cultural agenda. This itself was not a major problem for him. Rather, what bothered him the most was the arrogance and pride that some Western missionaries demonstrated. Kanzo often mentioned that not a single nation has even been saved entirely by foreign missionaries. On the contrary, missionaries often destroyed countries instead of building them. From Mexico's Montezuma to the Peruvian Incan empires, Christianity's course has been one of absorption, destruction, and, in some cases even cultural annihilation. As he noted, Western Christendom kills non-Christian countries by introducing rum and whisky, and tobacco and by bringing with it its many foul diseases. Uchimura Kanzo believed that Roman Catholicism was only suited to the Roman and post-Roman culture; similarly, Anglican Christianity emerged from the English culture, and Lutheranism from Germany. So, why not have a Japanese Christianity that is fully compatible to both Japan and Jesus?

---

5 - Michelson, Carl. Japanese Contribution to Christian Theology. Philadelphia: The Westminster Press, 1960.

To this I would add the following: We have European Christianity in all its variations, why not African Christianity with all its colorful diversity? Or Asian or Indian? Gradually, Kanzo became a promoter of an independent church, free from control and financial bondage to the powers-that-be outside of Japan. Because he was so devoted to Jesus, Kanzo was often resented by his own people. He was equally misunderstood by Christians, because of his passion for Japan. As he said:

> *I love two Js and no third; one is Jesus, and the other is Japan. I do not know which I love more, Jesus or Japan. I am hated by my countrymen for Jesus' sake as foreign belief, and I am disliked by foreign missionaries for Japan's sake as national and narrow. Even if I lose all my friends, I cannot lose Jesus and Japan... Jesus and Japan; my faith is not a circle with one center; it is an ellipse with two centers. My heart and mind revolve around the two dear names. And I know that one strengthens the other; Jesus strengthens and purifies my love for Japan; and Japan clarifies and objectives my love for Jesus. Were it not for the two, I would become a mere dreamer, a fanatic, an amorphous universal man.*[6]

After more than a century, the ideas of Uchimura Kanzo are coming into vogue again. Often, Western Christianity enters other cultures with the express intent of pressing people to accept both Jesus and western culture. The result is that, for many centuries we have neglected indigenous cultures, seen them as mere pagans and idol worshippers. We have not given them room to express Jesus in their own cultural setting.

Christianity has approached other cultures with an arrogant attitude, very often as an aggressor and not a guest. Christians often believe they have been given the whole truth and so automatically

---

6 - Kanzo, Uchimura. Nihon o sukuu no Kirisutokyo: The Christianity Which Could Save Japan. Tokyo: Tokyo Dokuritsu Zasshi No. 30, May 5, 1899, in Works 7:59.

assume others possess no truth at all. If we behave as guests and have the appropriate attitude towards other cultures, we will soon witness the Great Commission being fulfilled. For this Gospel will be preached to all the nations and a nation is not merely a politically-crafted territory, but an ethnos, a cultural/religious/racial and ethnic entity. Even today, most of our theological curricula are based on Western points of view. When we talk about Church History, for example, we are basically talking about early and recent Western/European history.

What about the history of the Church in China, India, or Africa? When did these histories begin? Westerners introduced Christianity, tobacco and whisky in these places all at the same time. Or, did Christianity already exist in places like Ethiopia, Egypt, India, Persia and even Japan? Why do we not know about these things? We are either ignorant of these histories, or too ethnocentric to acknowledge that these nations have also had their own versions of Christianity—and they are not exactly the same as our Western traditions. Thus, I would insist that Church is neither Western nor Eastern. It is a global Kingdom, the Kingdom of God.

Dialogue with Other Religions

We often view other religions as threats, see them as enemies, and consider them ungodly and even demonic. We are often intimidated by them. In my opinion, when you know who you are, as a follower of Christ, there is no need to be intimidated. Where there is no intimidation, there is room for mutual respect and dialogue. Jesus Christ urged us to love our neighbors as we love ourselves and to do good to them. Thank God He did not ask us to love only Christians! Our neighbors are many, the atheist, the Buddhist, the Muslim, and the Hindus. In fact, I believe that just as human beings can be each other's neighbors, so, too, the world's religions are themselves as each other's neighbors. Islam is a neighbor to Christianity, Christianity to Buddhism and Buddhism to Hinduism.

Unfortunately, we as Christians have often treated other religions with arrogance and viewed them as anti-Christian. Indeed, we often describe ourselves as better than, superior to any other world religion. In my view, this attitude has to change. We have to listen to them, not from a position of hostility and defensiveness, but with a genuine interest in exchanging information on an equal basis, with due respect and love.

Only then will we be able to manifest Christ's love and His Good News to the world. All of these earlier religions and traditions, have once, in their own time and their own way, done some good for humanity. We may not ignore or eliminate them and then seek to replace them with Christianity. We believe that there is only one way to the Father, namely, through Jesus Christ. In our faith, there is no doubt about this. However, there are many ways to Jesus. I know of people who came to Jesus through reading the Koran, and some through Buddhism. Once again, I would like to emphasize that there is only one-way to the Father and it is through Jesus Christ. But what is the way to Jesus? There are thousands upon thousands of such ways, including religious and non-religious ideologies. As His missionaries, we should seek common ground with these religions and ideologies or cultures in order to co-assist them in coming to Christ. Instead of calling people to other religions, Jesus invited them to Himself. Therefore instead of hoping that other religions would be brought to "Christianity", let us bring Christ to them. That way they can culturally be who they are and still follow Jesus. One of my Japanese friends, Rev. Arimasa Kubo, used to give a very inspiring example:

> In autumn, in parts of Japan, one can find Japanese persimmon trees laden with orange-colored fruit. However, these trees are of two kinds: one that bears bitter fruit and another that bears sweet fruit—and both look identical. It is impossible to distinguish from the outside, which is which. The sweet fruit is delicious, but the bitter one is so disgusting that you surely

could not bear to eat it. When I find a bitter persimmon tree, I sometimes wish to cut it down. But, there is another, better way, namely to change it into a sweet one. You do this by cutting off a shoot from a sweet persimmon tree and grafting it onto the trunk of the bitter one; by the next year, the whole of the bitter tree will have changed and will produce sweet fruit. It is that easy. The same thing can be said of the Japanese religions. Too many modern missionaries coming from the West thought that Japanese Shinto and Buddhism were forms of paganism, bitter persimmon trees. They tried to cut down Shintoism and Buddhism, but until now, they have failed. If Christianity is reintroduced appropriately to the Japanese by being grafted onto Shintoism and Japanese Buddhism, the Japanese will become reconciled with Christ.[7]

---

7 - Lee, Samuel. Rediscovering Japan, Reintroducing Christendom: Two-Thousand Years of Christian History in Japan. Lanham: Hamilton Books, 2010.

A **New** Kind of Pentecostalism

Chapter Twelve

Dialogue with Islam

And if the Holy Spirit descend
In grace and power infinite
His comfort in these days to lend
To them that humbly wait on it,
Theirs too the wondrous works can be
That Jesus wrought in Galilee.

Hafez, Persian Poet
1320-1391

There are three monotheistic/Abrahamic religions in the world: Judaism, Christianity and Islam. They all claim to preach truth, peace, and love, yet each has brought more conflict to human history. From the persecutions of Christians by the Jews during the first century, to the persecutions of the Jews by Christians during the Middle Ages; from the siege of Jerusalem by the Muslims to its siege by the Crusaders in the Middle Ages; from the rude occupation of the Holy Land by Zionists to the evil tragedy of 9/11 and the current occupation of Palestine, the invasion of Iraq, the bombings in Bali, the terrorist attacks in Madrid . . . almost every conflict in the world is in one way or the other related to these religions.

The Original Conflict

It is generally believed that the roots of the Judaic/Christian/Islamic conflict can be found in the Old Testament and in the Torah. Jews, Christians and Muslims all agree that Abraham is the father of these three religions. All three believe that their religions came to existence through Abraham's lineage, hence the term 'Abrahamic.' They all agree that Abraham had two important sons, Ishmael and Isaac, born from different mothers. The centuries-long conflict between Jews and Arabs seems to be motivated by anger and revenge between the offspring of these two brothers.

Abraham loved Sarah dearly, but she was barren. However, God had promised Abraham that he would be a great nation, and that he would become the father of all the nations through Sarah's child:

> *Now Sarai, Abram's wife, had borne him no children. But she had an Egyptian maidservant named Hagar; so she said to Abram, "The Lord has kept me from having children. Go, sleep with my maidservant; perhaps I can build a family through her." Abram agreed to what Sarai said. So after Abram had been living in Canaan ten years, Sarai his wife took her Egyptian maidservant Hagar and gave her to her husband to be his wife. He slept with Hagar, and she conceived. When she knew she was pregnant, she began to despise her mistress. Then Sarai said to Abram, "You are responsible for the wrong I am suffering. I put my servant in your arms, and now that she knows she is pregnant, she despises me. May the Lord judge between you and me." "Your servant is in your hands," Abram said. "Do with her whatever you think best." Then Sarai mistreated Hagar; so she fled from her.*

Genesis 16:1–6

Sarah made a crucial mistake by not waiting on the Lord's promise. She was impatient and therefore acted in the flesh. This act of the flesh caused Abram to sleep with a maidservant from Egypt named Hagar. Hagar conceived a child, Ishmael. Later, Sarah out of jealousy mistreated Hagar. This caused Hagar to flee:

> *One day Hagar fled from Sarai. Afterward, the angel of the Lord appeared to Hagar and told her to go back to Sarai. He*

also said: "You are now with child and you will have a son. You shall name him Ishmael, for the Lord has heard of your misery. He will be a wild donkey of a man; his hand will be against everyone and everyone's hand against him, and he will live in hostility toward all his brothers."

Genesis 16:11–12

Notice the word "brothers" here. Brothers have the same father: in this case, the sons of Abraham, Isaac and Ishmael. Abraham was eighty-six years old when Ishmael was born. Twelve years later, God appeared to him and promised him Isaac, from whose line He would bless all the nations of the world. When Abraham was one hundred years old, Isaac was born to Sarah. Ishmael would have been fourteen at the time.

> *"The child grew and was weaned, and on the day Isaac was weaned Abraham held a great feast. But Sarah saw that the son whom Hagar the Egyptian had borne to Abraham was mocking, and she said to Abraham, "Get rid of that slave woman and her son, for that slave woman's son will never share in the inheritance with my son Isaac." This matter distressed Abraham greatly because it concerned his son. But God said to him, "Do not be distressed about the boy and your maidservant. Listen to whatever Sarah tells you, because it is through Isaac that your offspring will be reckoned. I will make the son of your maidservant into a nation also, because he is your offspring."*

Genesis 21:8–13

Sarah "used" her maidservant to bear a child for her. After God gave Sarah her own son, she no longer needed or wanted Hagar. At first, she called Hagar a maidservant, and later she called her a slave girl. She clearly mistreated her. This whole story has an important consequence: rejection and all of the implications thereof. Sarah

97

rejected Hagar when she did not need her anymore. What would be the consequences of such a rejection for the children of Ishmael? We still see them today: rejection brings forth hatred, anger, and eventually the drive to revenge.

This story involves two important women: Sarah and Hagar. Both of them were imperfect, both made many mistakes. But how can such wrongs be redressed? How can their consequences be reversed? How can these two nations be reconciled? Subsequently, conflicts arose between the descendants of Esau, who married Ishmael's daughter Basemath (Genesis 36:3), and the descendents of Jacob. Jacob (who is called Israel) cheated his brother and stole the birthright, thus creating still more enmity between these two brothers and their eventual offspring.

We may agree that what Sarah did was not right. Similarly for Jacob. And, clearly, these mistakes had consequences. Based on the scriptures, the story between Judaism and Islam is one of abuse, rejection, manipulation and fraud.

In Middle Eastern cultures, stories are kept alive by passing them down from generation to generation. Even though we now live thousands of years later these stories are still shared as are many other historical facts. Details that have been passed down through centuries have thrown more fuel on the fire of the ongoing dispute between these religions.

The Historical Conflict

Today's conflict is a kind of reinterpretation of the old one—rejection, abuse and betrayal—but it is unfolding under much more complex conditions. Long before Islam existed as a religion, the Ishmaelites existed as a tribe. They were the Arabs, as well as some of the Northern Galileans. But, even during the time of Jesus, there was conflict between the Galileans and the Judean Jews. To fundamentalists from Judea, the Galileans, were not considered pure since, after the Diaspora, they had intermarried with gentiles.

The conflict between the Jews and the Galileans or the Samaritans was not only based on ethnic issues, but also on theological ones. The story of the Samaritan woman and Jesus at the well of Jacob makes this clear:

> *"Sir," the woman said, "I can see that you are a prophet. Our fathers worshiped on this mountain, but you Jews claim that the place where we must worship is in Jerusalem." Jesus declared, "Believe me, woman, a time is coming when you will worship the Father neither on this mountain nor in Jerusalem. You Samaritans worship what you do not know; we worship what we do know, for salvation is from the Jews. Yet a time is coming and has now come when the true worshipers will worship the Father in spirit and truth, for they are the kind of worshipers the Father seeks. God is spirit, and his worshipers must worship in spirit and in truth." The woman said, "I know that Messiah" (called Christ) "is coming. When he comes, he will explain everything to us." Then Jesus declared, "I who speak to you am he."*
>
> John 4:20-26

It seems that the Samaritans and the Jews had a theological and traditional problem where the place of worship was concerned. Jews designated Jerusalem for this but the Samaritans did not. And, in the conflict between the three religions today, each claims that theirs is the true one, each holds that they have the right form of worship and know the right way to approach God. However, Jesus' reply to this sort of controversy was crucial. He said that we should not worship God in a certain place or a certain city, be it Jerusalem or Rome or anywhere else, but rather in spirit and in truth. This is something that we as Christians often forget. We tend to overemphasize geographical places like Jerusalem, instead of focusing on the Jerusalem in our hearts and longing for the spirit, for truth, righteousness, neighborly love, grace and mercy.

The Christianity that arose out of the non-violent resistance of the early believers was a threat to the established Jewish religious system. This is why the early persecutions of Christians were carried out by the Jewish religious establishments. Centuries later, Christianity entered the political arena and became the dominant religion of the Roman Empire and of Europe. But Christians persecuted Jews in major European cities, for the European Christianity of those days claimed that the Jews had killed Jesus. This for centuries was one of the theological foundations of anti-Semitic Europe, which culminated in the disastrous and tragic Holocaust that took millions of lives, including more than six million Jews. Luther's writings even reveal a tendency to anti-Semitism:

> *"I had made up my mind to write no more either about the Jews or against them. But since I learned that these miserable and accursed people do not cease to lure to themselves even us, that is, the Christians, I have published this little book, so that I might be found among those who opposed such poisonous activities of the Jews, who warned the Christians to be on their guard against them"*[1]

In his "little book" Luther advised, "If we wish to wash our hands of the Jews' blasphemy and not share in their guilt, we have to part company with them. They must be driven from our country," and "We must drive them out like mad dogs." This kind of language is reminiscent of Christian fanatics who speak evil of Muslims—and vice- versa.

The rise of Islam in the seventh century AD created still further conflicts. Early Islam was relatively peaceful. However, later on when it became an organized religion and became entangled in the political system of the Middle East, things began to change. In the early phase

---

1 - Luther's Works, Martin Bertram, trans., Philadelphia: Fortress Press, 1971, 47:137.

of its development, Islam was ambitious to share their faith with the world, and they did this largely by conquest. Within a short period of time, the Arabs had invaded vast parts of the Middle East, Northern Africa, Spain and other areas. Some parts of Africa still speak Arabic in preference to their native languages.

During the Arab conquest, one city was considered to be crucially important —Jerusalem. All three Abrahamic religions identified it as their holy city and claimed ownership of the land upon which it is built. This political stance, together with the various theological disputes that developed, caused the three religions to enter into war–a war which has continued ever since.

From the seventeenth to the nineteenth century, Christian Europe colonized half the world – and they did so for the sake of economic growth. The slave trade and the annexation of nations and territories was part of this expansion. Christianity often proceeded by force, as evidenced in the ethnic histories of places such as the Americas (North, Central, and South) and Africa. The result was profound physical, moral and emotional injury to whole races of peoples— and an ensuing resentment of Christianity. However, this has also created an opportunity for Islam to gain converts, especially among Africans, but also among African-Americans. Christian imperialism, accompanied by adventurism, caused the West to lose credibility among the peoples of the world. People's trust had been thoroughly breached. One further consequence of this is that Christianity has lost many members to other religions or even to atheism.

After centuries of European persecution, Zionism arose at the end of the nineteenth century when people claimed that God would restore Zion and bring back the scattered people of Israel to their historical and Biblical territory. The tragedy of the Holocaust of WWII gave the Zionist vision force and in 1948, the nation of Israel was founded. The Arabs and Palestinians, however, viewed this as a case of occupation of their land. The situation became worse with the rise of Evangelicalism in America as well as in the UK and Europe. The eschatological theologies of American Evangelicalism and Western Pentecostalism emphasize the link between the restoration of Israel as a nation and the time of the return of Jesus Christ. Some even believe that being opposed to the state of Israel means being against God. This theology has caused some wealthy Evangelicals to support Zionism. They have lobbied the American government heavily for support of Israel and in addition to this, Christian tourism began to flourish in the Middle East. This caused confusion among the Arabs. They once again lost trust in Christians who were now collaborating with the American superpower and neglecting the rights of the Palestinians. They seemed to forget that not all Palestinians are Muslims but that many are Christians.

The feelings of distrust increased again, during the Russian–Afghanistan war in the eighties, the West "used" (remember Sarah "used" Hagar, as mentioned earlier) the Muslims to fight against communism. Weapons were provided and, with Islam as its allies, the West financed wars against communism. After the fall of communism, those fundamentalist Muslims who were fighting the communists were no longer needed by the Western governments, so they gradually came to be defined as the enemy. Could it be that the cruel 9/11 attack was the result of centuries of frustration on the part of Muslims toward the West? Unfortunately, one instance of bloodshed seems to require another, so America attacked Afghanistan and, later, Iraq. Many innocent people died, among them Iraqis, Americans, Dutch, British, Indians, and many others.

Theological Conflict

Often people ask question whether Jews, Christians, and Muslims, even worship the same God. The answer is simple and yet complex. All three Abrahamic religions theoretically believe in the same God, based on the theology of the Old Testament: Both Ishmael and Israel are Abraham's sons, and God promised prosperity to both Ishmael and Israel. Thus, it is indeed the case that descendants of both Ishmael and Israel historically speaking, believe in the God. However, the revelational aspects of God are not the same. In other words, the image or the revelation these religions have about God is not the same. In this respect, Judaism and Islam are much closer together than either of them is to Christianity. Neither Islam nor Judaism has a revelation or understanding regarding Jesus Christ. However, it seems that even the majority membership of organized Christianity also does not have a clue as to who He is! Jesus Himself said that many would call him Lord, but that He would not recognize them.

Not everyone who says to me, "Lord, Lord," will enter the kingdom of heaven, but he who does the will of my Father who is in heaven will enter. Many will say to me on that day, "Lord, Lord, did we not prophesy in your name, and in your name cast out demons, and in your name perform many miracles?" And then I will declare to them, "I never knew you; depart from me, you who practice lawlessness."

Matthew 7:21-23

The Jews do not view Jesus as the Son of God or as the Messiah; Muslims believe He is the latter, but not the former. Belief in Jesus as the Son of God or as the Messiah cannot be pressed upon a person by evangelistic programs or formulas. One needs personal conviction, to undergo a change within in order to understand that Jesus Christ is the image of God, Immanuel, God who is with us, God who has become human. However, there is a distinction between the person of Jesus and the larger history of Christianity. Jesus came to love, forgive and redeem. Jesus loved all humans—the Jew and the Samaritan as well as the Roman, the oppressor. Jesus was a Jew raised in Galilee, in the region of Palestine, which was under the occupation of the Romans. Religiously and ethnically He was a Jew, but politically and geographically He was a Palestinian. Does this not provide some basis for claiming that there is a common ground between the faiths?

What can we do?

Change begins with us. The mind rationalizes what the heart decides. Therefore, truth based on rationality is relative, not absolute. We even quote the Bible based on what we have sought to justify. If we, as Christians, decide in our hearts to become bridge builders rather than function divisively, then we are on the right track. The solution to this age-old problem is to put aside doctrinal differences and begin to treat each other with respect. If we cannot communicate on a human level, we will not be able to achieve any sort of social solidarity or theological unity. God spoke to Abraham and promised that he would be the father of all nations, adding,

> *"I will bless those who bless you, and whoever curses you I will curse; and all peoples on earth will be blessed through you"*

Genesis 12:3

Most of our attention focuses on the second part of the verse: those who curse Abraham will be cursed. But, we often neglect the fact that God also called Abraham to be a blessing to others. This biblical fact itself can serve as the basis for achieving a common ground among the three Abrahamic religions. We are all called to be a blessing to each other instead of engaging in mutual ridicule and acts of violence in the name of God.

I love the story of Abraham and the treaty of Beersheba with Abimelech. Abraham and his people were guests in the land of Abimelech:

> *At that time Abimelech and Phicol, the commander of his forces, said to Abraham, "God is with you in everything you do. Now swear to me here before God that you will not deal falsely with me or my children or my descendants. Show to me and the country where you are living as an alien the same kindness I have shown to you." Abraham said, "I swear it." Then*

Abraham complained to Abimelech about a well of water that Abimelech's servants had seized. But Abimelech said, "I don't know who has done this. You did not tell me, and I heard about it only today." So Abraham brought sheep and cattle and gave them to Abimelech, and the two men made a treaty. Abraham set apart seven ewe lambs from the flock, and Abimelech asked Abraham, "What is the meaning of these seven ewe lambs you have set apart by themselves?" He replied, "Accept these seven lambs from my hand as a witness that I dug this well." So that place was called Beersheba, because the two men swore an oath there. After the treaty had been made at Beersheba, Abimelech and Phicol the commander of his forces returned to the land of the Philistines.

Genesis 21:22-34

As we can see here, although Abraham was a guest, he became mightier than even the original inhabitants of this area; yet, he swore an oath to not deal with Abimelech and his people falsely. This covenant was not only made for Abimelech's sake, but also for that of his descendants. And, such an approach should be taken by every guest and host. This is how humanity has to interact: to not deal with each other falsely or wrong each other. Abraham was an exquisite example. If humankind had done as he did, the Native Americans would still be on their lands, as would the Jews and Palestinians, and we would all be living together as neighbors, friends, brothers and sisters of humanity.

I hope that as followers of Christ we can learn to become bridge builders rather than provokers of conflict. Let us start to be more like Jesus, who loved/loves the Jews–a people oppressed by the Romans–but who also loved the Romans even though they were oppressors to many. He understood that oppressing others is a sign of weakness.

Let us love humanity instead of labeling people as pro- or anti-Israel.
In such a theology there is no place for zealots like Barabbas, who
held that military action was the way to redeem Israel from Roman
tyranny. In contrast, Jesus said,

"Love your enemies, bless those who curse you"

Matthew 5:42-45

Let us be bridge builders. Such people usually work at borders.
They bind together two opposed entities, two poles reminiscent of
the outstretched arms of Jesus Christ on the cross. Bridge builders
connect and reconcile places, peoples, hearts, classes, ethnicities,
cultures, and denominations. Bridge builders are always on the
edge, in danger of slipping, falling or injuring themselves. They
are misunderstood, even cursed by all parties to a conflict. Bridge
builders dare to speak out, to reach out where no one does. Every
society needs bridge builders. Perhaps you are one! Let our love for
humanity be greater than our own personal agendas and religious
ideologies. Let us promote life not only after death, but life now!
Today!

Chapter Thirteen

The True Pentecost
Promoting Justice

All the believers were one in heart and mind.
No one claimed that any of his possessions was his own,
but they shared everything they had. With great power the
apostles continued to testify to the resurrection of the Lord Jesus,
and much grace was upon them all.

There were no needy persons
among them. For from time to time those who owned
lands or houses sold them, brought the money from the sales
and put it at the apostles' feet, and it was distributed
to anyone as he had need.

Acts 4:32-35

In the past twelve chapters, I have been discussing possibilities for a New Kind of Pentecostalism. What I am longing for, what I desire, is hardly new! It started on the day of Pentecost, as we read in the book of Acts. Pentecostalism has always been on the margins of religious life. It therefore has to once again be the promoter of Justice as in the days of the apostles. Immediately after their intense experience of Pentecost, when the disciples were filled with Holy Spirit, Peter stood up boldly and quoted from the prophet Joel:

Then Peter stood up with the eleven, raised his voice and
addressed the crowd: "Fellow Jews and all of you who live in
Jerusalem, let me explain this to you; listen carefully to what I

*say. These people are not drunk, as you suppose. It's only nine in
the morning! No, this is what was spoken by the prophet Joel:*

*"In the last days, God says, I will pour out my Spirit on all
people. Your sons and daughters will prophesy, your young men
will see visions, your old men will dream dreams. Even on my
servants, both men and women, I will pour out my Spirit in
those days, and they will prophesy. I will show wonders in the
heavens above and signs on the earth below, blood and fire and
billows of smoke. The sun will be turned to darkness and the
moon to blood before the coming of the great and glorious day
of the Lord. And everyone who calls on the name of the Lord
will be saved.' "Fellow Israelites, listen to this: Jesus of Nazareth
was a man accredited by God to you by miracles, wonders and
signs, which God did among you through him, as you yourselves
know."*

Acts 2:14-22

Almost every point Peter made here was realized through the
experience of Pentecost. Many of us rightfully emphasize the outpouring of the Holy Spirit and the official birth of the Church of
Jesus Christ as having occurred years ago on the day of the original
Pentecost, however, I believe that there are other less simplistic
answers to the question of the importance of Pentecost.

Pentecost, the Diversity of Races and Cultures

First of all, Pentecost is about honoring diversity of races and
cultures. It is about people (In the last days, God says, I will pour out
my Spirit on all people.") Jesus Christ came to restore us to the Father;
the Holy Spirit came to restore us to each other. That is why, on the
day of Pentecost, the people from various nations heard the disciples
praying in tongues, they all heard them in their own language: the
Arabs in Arabic, the Persian in Farsi, the Turk, the Chinese, the

Egyptian etc. And, indeed, on that day Peter preached about the outpouring of the Holy Spirit upon all mankind!

Pentecost is about ethnic diversity! It dealt with racial barriers, so now the gospel is not only for Israel, but for all. Today there are many hidden forms of racism in the church. We often talk about loving other cultures and races, but deep in our hearts there are prejudices and various forms of bias: "I love the blacks, as long as they keep their distance," Or, "well I love the Arabs, that is why I am going there to fix them with Christ." This kind of language is loaded with hidden meanings and agendas. Again, I would underscore the fact that Pentecost is about unity in diversity. We are the colors of God. We all are His children and we have to make sure that all races, all ethnicities are loved. If the Church allows such prejudices to persist, what can we possibly expect from the world? I consider myself a very blessed man, because I am originally from the Middle East, grew up in Europe, married a Korean woman, studied sociology specializing in Japanese culture, and I minister to Filipinos, Nigerians and Ghanaians. This is all deeply enriching and inspiring.

Pentecost and the recognition thereof should be a battle against all forms of racism and prejudice. This is the spirit of that miraculous day. As I mentioned earlier, prejudice, discrimination and racism do unfortunately mark our religious life. Most of the time when we speak of such things we often think of the racist attitudes of the white man toward non-whites. However, racism and discrimination are also very pronounced among non-white Christians as well. Overall, we need a cleansing of hearts. Major surgery is necessary to rectify such problems because they separate us from the Spirit of God. Even though the world's cultures are diverse, each one has good and bad features. We have to avoid bad or negative aspects of each, and take the good ones and learn from each other. Gradually we can develop the sort of religious culture that Christ called us to, meaning that people will be gentle, humble, kind, and loving. These are the character traits of a Christian. The Holy Spirit cannot dwell in a heart that entertains hidden prejudices and allows itself to hold racist attitudes towards others.

Pentecost, Vision & Dreams

Secondly, Pentecost is about hope, visions and dreams. That is what the prophet Joel prophesied concerning that day. The Holy Spirit came to give us strength and power to believe and hope, to dream about goodness, righteousness, dignity, integrity and unconditional love towards people and all of creation. Pentecost promises hope, where there is none, when, diseases, viruses, epidemics, natural calamities, wars and crime are all destroying our world. The Holy Spirit empowers us to have the vision to rebuild, restore, care and love! As Bishop Tutu said, 'Christianity is about helping God to fulfill His dreams for humanity and creation.' This is the essence of Pentecost! Or, at least that is how it ought to be understood!

Pentecost and Gender Equality

Thirdly, Pentecost is about celebrating women, our mothers, sisters and daughters! It is about equality between men and women in society, in the family, at work and in church. In the Acts of the Apostles, Peter quoted the words of the prophet Joel who said that, in the last days, both men and women who are equally servants of God will prophesy (Acts 2:18). For centuries and even today in many places in the world, women are being oppressed by men. Unfortunately men such as I am myself, have forgotten where we come from, that we are the seed of woman. Today, we speak about the rights of the women in other nations, in the Arab or Islamic world. We rightfully criticize these nations for how they treat their women. What about ourselves? Does our western society truly respect women's freedom? What have consumerism and capitalistic society done to them except make them into objects of lust? Is this freedom?

We despise some religions and cultures for how they put women in veils but what about all of the pornography/sex magazines and websites in the West? Women who are involved in this are victims of a consumer society that is based on greed and undisciplined desires. We have forgotten that these women are someone's daughters, sisters, and or mothers. So many women suffer so greatly. The church should love, respect and honor them but, often it is actually in the seeming spirit of Pentecost that we see injustice done to them. We as the Pentecostal Church have to help our sisters regardless of who they are and what sort of background they come from. I would argue that Pentecostalism can play a very important role in helping to raise the standard of women in both society and the church. During the early years after the Pentecostal revival of 1906, the majority of the converts were female. They were active as evangelists, preachers and pastors and even they taught at Bible schools or ran their own.

Unfortunately, this gradually changed when Pentecostalism become an organized religion. Denominations developed and theological doctrines were worked out. These led to disagreements on various levels, and one of them was the role of women in the church.

Pentecostals who are influenced by such conservative ideas believe that teaching or exercising authority over a man in the church is not biblically correct. This includes both preaching from the pulpit and administrative work. They often quote the following scriptures from (1 Timothy 2:12-15; 1 Timothy 3:1) in support of their position:

> *But I do not allow a woman to teach or exercise authority over a man, but to remain quiet. For it was Adam who was first created, and then Eve. And it was not Adam who was deceived, but the woman being quite deceived, fell into transgression. But women shall be preserved through the bearing of children if they continue in faith and love and sanctity with self-restraint.*

1 Timothy 2:12-15

111

On the other hand, in the past two decades there have been some positive changes in Pentecostalism. As compared to other evangelical denominations and to other established monotheistic religions, we can see now that, relatively speaking, Pentecostalism has given women the place they rightfully deserve; women are being ordained as pastors, bishops, prophetesses and apostles. Ordination, when it is combined with educational programs, can be very liberating and inspiring for women outside Pentecostal circles. In the Middle East and in some Asian countries, we see Pentecostal women leaders impacting their societies, despite the various forms of oppression that they suffer.

Lastly, when I speak about equality between men and women in church leadership, this does not mean that I agree with every woman minister on major issues. There are as many corrupt female leaders in the Pentecostal movement as there are male ones. Corrupt leadership does not recognize gender. There are female pastors, leaders and especially female apostles in our world today who did not have proper education, lack character and integrity and try to imitate their counterparts.

The Pentecost and Evangelism

Pentecost is a mission! It means sharing the good news with others around us. Peter preached the gospel to 3000 people on the day of Pentecost. These 3000 men then returned to their nations and preached it to multitudes as well. However, sometimes I think that our mission and sharing of the gospel has not been as effective as it is supposed to be. Recently, I have begun to grasp something which I believe may be important in this connection: as long as we approach people, nations and cultures with our hidden agendas, we cannot be truly successful in our missionary work. We cannot genuinely share the gospel. Often in the past, missionary work has been corrupted by political interests and hidden economic agendas. One striking example of this is colonialism and the slave trade in Africa – all of which was carried out by so-called Christians, by religious groups from the West trying to bring the "gospel" to these people. There were, of course, many Europeans whose intentions were genuine but there were far more people who had agendas other than preaching the gospel. On the individual level, we unconsciously may do the same thing. We intentionally want to be someone's friend in order to convert him / her to Christianity. No matter how good one's intentions are, there is still operative in one's consciousness a hidden agenda, namely to turn someone into a Christian!

When that person does not fit into our personal agenda, or is not receptive to what we want to say, we set them aside and move on to someone else! The basic principle which ought to guide mission work and sharing of the gospel is to have a genuine and true unconditional love for the person, people or nation you are engaging. It is not we who make people Christians, or followers of Christ, but rather the Holy Spirit who moves them. All we have to do is to share Christ's unconditional love and reveal it to mankind. We also have to rethink our vocabulary. Words like 'converting people' are no longer appropriate. People are not "software" or "files" to be converted into another format! And, we often say things like: "I helped him to be converted to Christianity." I rather prefer the word reconciliation: We become reconciled to God, not converted to a religion! Or we speak about he / she having 'found' Christ! Christ was not lost! We are the ones who are! Humanity itself is lost! Our job is not to bring a person to Christ, but bring Christ to the person. Christ can only go to someone when we are willing to be there as well. Remember that Christ came into this world; we did not go to Him. Pentecost is about coming to that place where Christ would be! That is the essence of our mission.

Social Justice

Lastly, Pentecost means a commitment to social action! Evangelism and mission cannot be completed in the absence of a sense of social justice. In the Book of Acts (2), we read that the believers devoted themselves to prayer and fellowship and those who had worldly goods sold what they had and gave it to those who had less so that they had all things in common. Only the Holy Spirit can help us to share life like this. I realize that communism adapted this idea but its theorists excluded the role of faith from their program. They ignored the message of love manifested by Christ as well as the transformative power of the Holy Spirit.

The Prophet Amos formulates this correctly, when he conveys the message of justice to his contemporary Israelites:

> *Woe to you who long for the day of the LORD! Why do you long for the day of the LORD? That day will be darkness, not light. It will be as though a man fled from a lion only to meet a bear, as though he entered his house and rested his hand on the wall only to have a snake bite him. Will not the day of the LORD be darkness, not light—pitch-dark, without a ray of brightness? "I hate, I despise your religious festivals; your assemblies are a stench to me. Even though you bring me burnt offerings and grain offerings, I will not accept them. Though you bring choice fellowship offerings, I will have no regard for them. Away with the noise of your songs! I will not listen to the music of your harps. But let justice roll on like a river, righteousness like a never-failing stream.*

Amos 5:18-24

Amos rightfully spoke about those believers who were longing for the end of the days, or what we today call "end times." They were so preoccupied with eschatological doctrines, festivals and religious gatherings that they neglected the poor and the suffering, especially the orphans, the widows and the migrants. This reminds me of some Pentecostal circles in which people are either too busy preaching about end times and damning people to hell, or have turned the church into a festival or a show where little attention is paid to social justice and care for the poor. Both early church Pentecostalism as well as the Azusa Revival stimulated action for social justice. I will never forget the story of an Asian sister, a migrant and domestic worker, who was made pregnant by her employer, a married man. When her belly began to grow, he dumped her out of the house. It was winter, Christmas time. She had nowhere to go. She called the various Pentecostal churches for help. Instead of helping her, one church started preaching at her about hell and adultery. They scared her away. Another told her that she had to be delivered because she was possessed of demons. Thank God she called my friends. They picked her up and helped her give birth. The father never acknowledged the child but she has been coming to church regularly and is being cared for by the community. Why is the door of the church closed to those who are in need? Why do we automatically label them sinners? How can we judge people without even knowing their stories? It may be that this particular sister was sexually harassed or even raped–we do not know, yet we act as if we do. Who are we to shut the door of justice to people whom we call sinners? Let us not become preoccupied with our nice-sounding worship songs, youth camps and Hollywood style conferences, and, at the same time, neglect the poor and the oppressed. As I minister among the most fragile migrants in Amsterdam, I can assure you that even today in twenty-first century Europe, there are people who live like Anne Frank.

In the Netherlands, I am daily confronted with many Asians and Africans who have left home and been living abroad for many years so as to work and send money back to their countries. There are various motivations, e.g., education of their children, care of a parent, paying the hospital bills for family member. Many left home hoping that after one or two years they would be returning but one or two years turned into ten or twenty. They have struggled mightily in order to get into a European country but then found that they were not eligible for a residence permit and so had to remain there illegally. Many of them ended up cleaning, doing domestic work for the average European working parents who often do not have the time to give to their children. Probably their job is more important, or the luxury of a two-income household does not permit them to have quality time with their kids, so they need domestic workers to take care of them!

But this is the case not only in the domestic household sector, but almost in every sector of so called "low profile work". These migrants are active in diverse areas such as agriculture and construction. These "undocumented" individuals are providing an enormous service to society and yet they are "invisible." What if they all stopped working at once? Western society, Europe in particular, would definitely be affected by their absence.

Some of our African, Asian and South American friends, and people from elsewhere as well, are suffering in Europe for reasons that many would not suspect. In the past year, I myself have witnessed how many have been brutally arrested and deported to their native countries; worst of all, they were treated as criminals. I regularly visit some homes and what I see is terrible: at least six to eight people live together in a house with only one room. All over the floor there are blankets, pillows, etc. Once someone rings the doorbell, fear fills these people's hearts—it could be the immigration police! Or, when someone even looks at them a bit suspiciously, their knees shake out of fear.

As a Christian leader, and a social activist, it is my duty to help those in need; people who have dreams of being happy just like you and me. As Christians, churches and ministries let us reach out to these people and provide help where it is needed. The true Pentecost is concerned with the poor, the oppressed, orphans, widows, and migrants. There is such gross social and economic imbalance—injustice and maldistribution of wealth—in the world. Are you sharing what you have with others who don't have what they need?

Chapter Fourteen

A **New** Kind of Pentecostalism

"Making the beginning is one third of the work."

An Irish Proverb

After reading what you have just read (or maybe following me on my blog), you may feel inclined to ask, "Is Samuel still a Pentecostal?" Indeed, I am, but I wholeheartedly believe that the Pentecostal movement needs serious reform. Just like any other religious movement, it has its own blind spots and makes its own errors, yet, at the same time, it shines in its own beauty. Whenever I say that I am a Pentecostal, I do not mean that I belong to a Pentecostal religious system, organization, or denomination. Instead, I believe in the very essence, the very foundation of our faith as it is based in the Pentecost documented in the Book of Acts. Also, I very much believe in the experiences I had eighteen years ago. What follows are some points by way of summary and conclusion.

I am a Pentecostal because I believe in the power of the Holy Spirit as it was revealed in the Bible, but also as He is still at work in our world today. Nevertheless, I do not agree with some of my Pentecostal friends who use the name of the Holy Spirit in a simplistic and even abusive way, i.e., to engage in a form of ethical escapism, as license to do and say what they want. The Holy Spirit is part of the Triune Godhead and simultaneously a power or a spiritual force. Indeed, this force is love. As noted, the greatest sign of the Holy Spirit is the power of love! Love is indeed a power; it forgives, liberates, and heals. The Holy Spirit empowers us to love even the unlovable, to reach the unreachable.

I am a Pentecostal because I believe in and emphasize the miracles of the Holy Spirit. I cannot deny them. I have seen with my own eyes people healed from sicknesses, some even instantly, when others prayed for them. At the same time, I disagree with some of my fellow Pentecostal friends who merchandize the works of the Holy Spirit. The commercialization of His miracles is sacrilegious. I disagree with the overemphasis on miracles, signs, and wonders, at the expense of justice and the righteousness for the poor and oppressed. I disagree with those who practice Pentecostalism while their own personal character shows little or no sign of the fruits of the Holy Spirit. I disagree with those who pretend to be super Pentecostals but do not know how to treat their spouses, neighbors, or children. True Pentecost-experience changes our characters and leads us to humility, grace, peace, and love. These are as important as signs and wonders.

I am a Pentecostal and do indeed believe in the Holy Spirit, but I do not believe that the Pentecostal denomination or churches have exclusive rights to His spiritual powers. Rather, the Holy Spirit is free to move among any Christ-loving church or denomination. I am a Pentecostal, but this does not make me superior to any other brothers and sisters from different denominations. I am a Pentecostal, but I do not tolerate any arrogance among those who claim to be Pentecostal. I honor all denominations that love Jesus Christ. Because I am a Pentecostal, I have learned to respect all of my brothers and sisters around the globe. Many of my friends are from other denominations or from the non-denominational realm.

I am a Pentecostal, and I believe that the Bible is an inspired work of the Holy Spirit; yet, I am also aware that human beings also wrote it. Further, some aspects of the Bible must be understood in historical and cultural context. I am a Pentecostal, but I disagree with some of my fellow Pentecostals who recklessly quote the Bible out of context and hurt others by doing so, or use Scripture to manipulate and control others for various reasons. I disagree with those who use the

Scriptures without love or consideration. For example, I disapprove of the homosexual lifestyle, but I am also aware of this ongoing issue in our society. I do not like to beat others over the head with a doom and gloom message by taking a "thus says the Bible" approach. If we do this, we are also condemning ourselves because it gives us many guidelines for living properly. If we choose to be judgmental, the very judgment rod that we use will become the measure of our worth. Do we judge others using the Bible? If so, then we ourselves will be so measured—a rather daunting prospect. I do not approve of perversity in any way, nor do I tolerate it. Nevertheless, I am always searching for wisdom and understanding in dealing with this sensitive subject.

I am a Pentecostal, but I disagree with my Pentecostal friends who quote the scriptures to enrich themselves financially. I am not against blessings or prosperity. At the same time, I do not condone the manipulative and exaggerated methods of fundraising or tithe-collection that are used by some men and women who claim to be Pentecostal. Unfortunately some televangelists have gone too far with this. I disagree with and disapprove of such acts done in the name of Pentecostalism.

I am a Pentecostal, and I indeed believe in the end times and the second coming of our Lord Jesus Christ. Yet, I disagree with some of my fellow Pentecostals who think along these lines. I am against commercializing eschatology. Our end-time theologies can have fatal consequences in our dealings with other people and other nations! In the name of end times, we easily label others as antichrists and justify our hateful actions towards them. I am certain that Jesus Christ is coming back; in fact, this is the foundation of my faith. However, I can never preach with 100% certainty how and when this will occur. Only He knows.

I am a Pentecostal because the Pentecost honors racial and cultural diversity. The Pentecost is fundamentally about people. Jesus Christ came to restore us to the Father; the Holy Spirit came to restore us to each other. Therefore, on the day of Pentecost, people from all nations under heaven were present, and when they heard the disciples praying in foreign tongues, they each heard the message in their own language, i.e., the Arabs in Arabic, the Persians in Farsi. Peter preached on that day about the outpouring of the Holy Spirit upon all people!

I am a Pentecostal because the Pentecost is about hope, visions, and dreams. Indeed, the prophet Joel prophesied that such things would occur on the day of Pentecost. On that day, the Holy Spirit came to give all of us the strength and power to believe and hope, to dream about goodness, righteousness, dignity, integrity, and unconditional love towards people and creation. Pentecost gives hope where there is no hope. When people, nations, diseases, viruses, epidemics, natural calamities threaten to ruin the world, we are given the power of vision to rebuild, restore, care, and love! As Bishop Tutu said, Christianity is about helping God to fulfill His dreams for humanity and creation. That is Pentecost! At least that is what it ought to be.

I am a Pentecostal because Pentecost is the day of equality for all mothers, daughters, and sisters! It is about equality between men and women in the Church. In the Acts of the Apostles, Peter quoted the words of the prophet, Joel, who mentioned that God said in the last days both men and women, His servants, would prophesy (Acts 2:18). For centuries women have been oppressed, and even today in many places in the world they continue to suffer discrimination and be denied equal rights with men. Unfortunately, men like myself have forgotten where we come from; i.e., we are the seed of the woman. Today, we speak about the rights of women in other nations, for example in the Arab or Islamic world. We criticize these nations' treatment of their women. But, what about ourselves? Does Western society truly respect the freedom of women? What have our consumerism and capitalistic society done to them? It has reduced them to objects of lust. Is this true freedom?

I am a Pentecostal because Pentecost means sharing and participating in social action! In the Book of Acts (2), we read that the believers devoted themselves to prayer and fellowship. Those who possessed many worldly goods sold what they had and gave their resources to those who had less. So, did they come to hold all things in common? The true Pentecost is concerned for the poor, the oppressed, the orphans, the widows, and the migrants. Our world is full of imbalance, injustice, and problems deriving from the improper distribution of wealth. It is the duty of the Church to rise up and do something about poverty, illness, and injustice. We must share what we have with others.

I believe that, if we do not change our lifestyle and correct our collective moral and ethical mistakes, the Pentecostal movement will lose ground in the Western world. We need a reformation within the movement. Other branches of Christianity have found themselves in a similar predicament in the past and reform movements have corrected the existing problems.

Lastly to my Non-Pentecostal friends, I would say; give the Pentecostalism the benefit of the doubt and hear us out! Unfortunately, because of the noise generated by some "super" Pentecostals, you cannot or—choose not—to hear the voices of the real ones. Engage in fellowship with us as we want to with you. Let us learn from each other! Not every aspect of Christianity can be explained in strictly theological terms. And, some things cannot be explained either in this way or scientifically, but they can indeed be described as evidence of the movement of the Holy Spirit. Moreover, they are explainable through the mysticism of His love and His work. Pentecostals have great things to offer the Christian world, the body of Christ; but, at the same time, they should reform their own ways, address their own faults, and learn to listen to others, especially to fellow believers from different denominations.

This is only the beginning of a phase of greater change that is sweeping across the world. It is the beginning of a Pentecostalism that goes back to the book of Acts. We are moving toward a New Kind of Pentecostalism, one of returning to the ancient values of the original Pentecostal event in a postmodern setting —in the global village. We are coming upon a new era.

Time is giving birth to **A New Kind of Pentecostalism.**

A **New** Kind of Pentecostalism

a tentative statement of faith

A **New** Kind of Pentecostalism

A Tentative Statement of Faith

The New Kind of Pentecostals are . . .

1. Those who do not claim that the Holy Spirit is the exclusive property of a particular denomination or church.

2. Those who respect other Christian denominations and traditions, and are willing to engage in fellowship, share and cooperate with them.

3. Those who believe that the unconditional love that is inspired and directed by the Holy Spirit is the greatest sign of our being filled with the Holy Spirit.

4. Those who share the Good News with all mankind, but in a manner full of grace and love and not out of arrogance and with a "we-know-better-than-you-attitude . . . "

5. Those who believe that miracles, signs and wonders are still possible today, but that one should not elevate these above the humility and message of Jesus Christ. They are the ones who are against commercializing and merchandizing the gifts and signs of the Holy Spirit.

6. Those who do not tolerate any form of fear-theology and manipulation in the name of the Holy Spirit in order to gain wealth, even for the ministry.

7. Those who believe in the grace that is in giving tithes and offerings, but are against abusive and manipulative forms of preaching (e.g., by using Malachi 3:8). Tithes and offerings should not be demanded, but must come from the heart of the giver. Fear preached from the pulpit provides neither proper incentive nor honest result.

8. Those who may disapprove of the non-heterosexual lifestyle, but are not witch-hunting homosexuals. Instead of using hateful vocabulary toward homosexuals, they listen to and pray for them.

9. The New Kind of Pentecostals are those who aim to play the role of bridge builders between the Jews and Palestinians. For God loves both of them . . .

10. Those who are not only concerned with miracles, signs and wonders, but are also concerned with social justice, and with the welfare of the poor, the oppressed, the orphans, the widows and the immigrants.

11. Those who respect other cultures as well as people's convictions and religious commitments, and so are willing to enter into dialogue with them without any hidden agendas.

12. Those who respect and have an ongoing dialogue with other cultures, yet are willing to take a critical stance on the types of inhumane practices that exist within these cultures.

13. Those who are concerned with the environment and are willing to provide Pentecostal input in caring for the creation.

14. Those who believe in the Bible as the inspired collection of Holy Scriptures, yet use the scriptures to bring forth grace and mercy and offer blessings instead of a doom and gloom theology.

15. Those who believe that leadership should be service to mankind, i.e., that leaders should serve instead of being served. They should sacrifice instead of demanding sacrifice. Leadership should be based on love and fellowship and not on rank.

16. Those who respect traditional churches, or organized religions, but believe that the real church is built of people and their relationship with God and with each other. They believe that the church is not a "building", but it is evidence of God's continually perfecting His kingdom.

A **New** Kind of Pentecostalism